Essential Visual Basic 4.0 *Fast*
Everything you need to know to develop applications in VB4

Springer

London
Berlin
Heidelburg
New York
Barcelona
Budapest
Hong Kong
Milan
Paris
Santa Clara
Singapore
Tokyo

John Cowell

Essential Visual Basic 4.0 *Fast*

How to Develop
Applications in
Visual Basic

With 157 Figures

Springer

John Cowell, BSc (Hons), MPhil, PhD
Department of Computer and Information Sciences
De Montfort University
Kents Hill Campus, Hammerwood Gate, Kents Hill
Milton Keynes, MK7 6HP, UK

ISBN-13: 978-3-540-19998-4   e-ISBN-13: 978-1-4471-3093-2
DOI: 10.1007/978 -1-4471-3093-2

British Library Cataloguing in Publication Data
Cowell, John R.
   Essential Visual Basic 4.0 fast : how to develop applications in Visual Basic
   1. Visual Basic (Computer program language)   2. Programming (Electronic computers)
   I. Title
   005.2'62

Library of Congress Cataloging-in-Publication Data
Cowell, John R.
   Essential Visual Basic 4.0 fast : how to develop applications in Visual Basic / John Cowell.
      p.   cm.
   Includes index.

   1. BASIC (Computer program language)   2. Microsoft Visual BASIC.
I. Title.
QA76.73.B3C685   1996
005.265–dc20   96-10945

Typeset from disk by T&A Typesetting Services, Rochdale

34/3830-543210 Printed on acid-free paper

Contents

1

Why Use Visual Basic?

Why Use Visual Basic?

Windows 95 is set to become the best-selling piece of software of all time; it is now the standard on all PCs. Visual Basic has sold over 30,000 copies, and sales are continuing at a rapid rate. If you are developing software either as a professional programmer, a student or for fun, it is very probable that you will be working in a Windows 95 environment, and if you are developing Windows 95 software you need Visual Basic.

Visual Basic offers a complete development environment for producing professional-standard applications. The environment is very intuitive to use, and if you already have some programming experience you can expect to use Visual Basic confidently after a few weeks' practice and with proficiency after about 2 months. Most experienced programmers find they prefer the Visual Basic environment to using languages such as C. Inexperienced programmers who meet Visual Basic as their first language find it a great development environment, and are often horrified if they later have to switch to some other language that lacks the features and ease of use of Visual Basic.

Visual Basic allows you to develop programs with the same professional heavyweight feel as the best-selling programs sold by Microsoft and others for hundreds of pounds. Recently, many third-party suppliers have started supplying "add-ons" to Visual Basic, so making it even easier to write software for your application. The chances are that whatever you want to do in a Windows environment, Visual Basic will let you do it.

One annoying imperfection in Visual Basic for British users is that there are a number of American spellings such as "Dialog". In order to avoid confusion, I have used the American spellings in cases like this, otherwise I have kept to British conventions.

Is This Book For You?

This book assumes that you have no prior knowledge of Visual Basic and provides an introduction to the language. It is also suitable for those at an intermediate level who want to learn how to develop serious, professional applications. It is assumed that you have some experience of using such Windows programs as word processors, spreadsheets and databases.

It is helpful if you already have some programming experience, but all the essential elements of the Visual Basic language are covered. If you have used BASIC before, especially variants such as QuickBASIC or QBasic, you will be able to switch to Visual Basic without any problems.

Visual Basic is supplied with better-than-average manuals and the usual high standard of on-line Help. These are fine if you have a good grasp of Visual Basic and need to look up a specific point. What the manuals and Help are not very good at, is providing is a readable, impartial guide to the language and environment. This book does not cover every minor detail of Visual Basic in the same way as the manuals, but it does give you a grasp of all the most important features of the language. There are many illustrations and examples. The best way to learn Visual Basic is to try out the examples for yourself.

How to Use This Book

You can use this book as a guide, starting at the beginning and working through to the end, or just look at individual chapters if you already have some experience of Visual Basic. How projects are organised and the essential features of the language are covered in the first part of the book, while more advanced topics such as using databases and object linking and embedding are covered later. This book is not intended to be a definitive in-depth description of Visual Basic – if it was it would be about ten times as long and take twenty times as long to read. The philosophy of the book is to cover a broad range of most of the key features of Visual Basic. Most people find that at first they don't need to learn everything about the language to be able to develop useful programs. If, for example, your first Visual Basic program does not use grids, you do not need to read the chapter on grids in order to start. The best way to use the book is to read the sections you need and to try the examples. One of the pleasures of Visual Basic is that it allows you to develop applications fast – you do not even need to read all of this book before you can start!

New Features in Version 4

This book is based on Version 4 – the latest version. Software developed using earlier revisions is compatible with this version. Version 4 is a significant advance over Version 3. The main additional features that have been added are:

- Improved database access. Database access was first included in Version 3, but it did not have the same intuitive feel as most aspects of Visual Basic. The user interface has been greatly improved in the latest version.
- There is a new language engine – Visual Basic for applications. This is fully compatible with the version of Basic in earlier releases, and also with Visual Basic in MS Project Version 4.0 and MS Excel Version 5.0.
- The context-sensitive Help has been greatly improved.
- A real problem in earlier version was that program lines could be very long. Visual Basic 4 has a line continuation character.
- There are some additional data bound controls, for example, list and combo boxes.
- The menu designer has been improved.
- The Data Form Designer has been added, which is a fast way of creating forms for accessing and amending database tables.
- **For Each...Next** and **With...End With** constructs are available in the Visual Basic.
- The menu bar has been significantly changed to carry out the same operations more easily, and the menu commands are grouped differently from earlier versions.

All the material covered in this book is part of both the standard and professional versions of Visual Basic. The major differences between the two versions (apart from the large increase in price) are that the Professional version has several additional features, for example, the Animated buttons and the 3-D controls.

What Computer You Need to Run Visual Basic

Computers are never fast enough and rarely have enough disk space or memory, so the faster and more powerful your computer the better. Realistically, though, Visual Basic can be run with quite a modest configuration and still provide reasonable performance. The minimum that you need so that the performance is adequate is:

- Intel 80486dX2 or better
- 8 MB or more of memory
- 50 MB of disk space for a full installation

Visual Basic runs successfully on the minimum configuration, however it does not run fast unless you have a higher specification computer. There are great improvements in performance using a Pentium with 16 MB of memory. The most critical feature is memory rather than processor speed. If you want to run Visual Basic at the same time as other Windows software, you should have even more memory than this to reduce the amount of swapping between disk and memory, as this process is much slower than when referring to memory alone.

Conventions

There are a few conventions used in this book which make it easier to read:

- All program examples are in italics
- All reserved words such as **For...Next** are in **bold** and start with a capital letter
- All user-defined names such as *MyFile* are in *italics*.

Running Visual Basic

The Visual Basic user interface seems complicated to use at first sight. There are several windows, each with its individual use. In this chapter you will learn about:

- Starting the Visual Basic program.
- The Visual Basic form.
- The toolbox window.
- The project window.
- The properties window.
- The project window.
- The menu bar.
- How to write a program.

Starting Visual Basic

When you have installed Visual Basic, all the icons that you need are put into a single folder, as shown in fig. 1.1.

- Click on **Start** on the taskbar.
- Click on the **Programs** option in the first menu.
- Click on the **Visual Basic 4** option in the second menu.
- Click on the **Visual Basic 4** option in the third menu displayed.

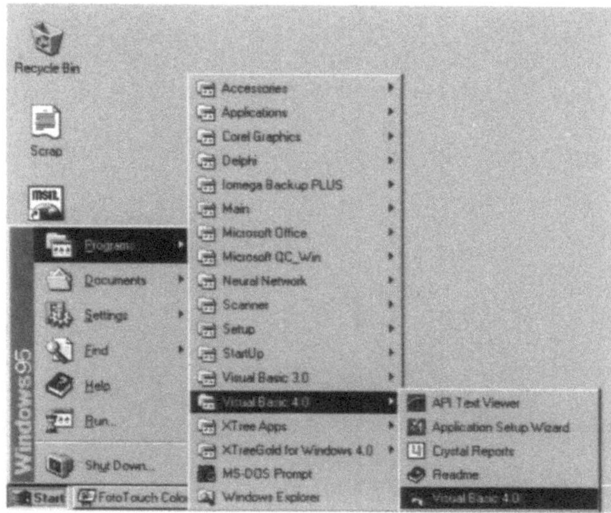

Fig. 1.1
Running Visual Basic (1).

An alternative way is to:

- Click on **Start** on the taskbar
- Click on the **Programs** option
- Click on Windows Explorer
- Search for vb32.exe as shown in fig. 1.2.

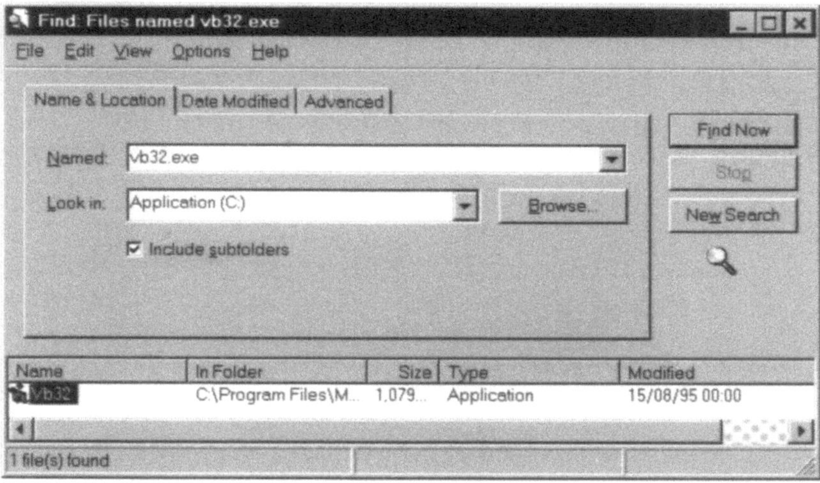

Fig. 1.2   *Running Visual Basic (2).*

When Visual Basic runs, it overlays whatever is on the screen so it is beneficial to have minimised any other applications. You can do this by clicking the right mouse button on a blank part of the taskbar and choosing **Minimise All Windows** from the pop-up menu.

You can restore a minimised window by clicking on the required window in the taskbar.

Before You Start...

Visual Basic has an excellent set of help tutorials that will give you an idea of what Visual Basic is capable of. They are useful if you have not used Visual Basic before. To run these tutorials, select the **Learn Microsoft Visual Basic** option from the **Help** menu on the toolbar. (If you do not know what the toolbar is, look ahead to Chapter 3).

The Visual Basic Design Screen

When you run Visual Basic for the first time the design screen, similar to the one shown in fig. 1.3, appears. The immediate reaction is to panic! The screen looks complicated, but it is surprising straightforward to use. It comprises a set of windows, each of which can be resized and moved around.

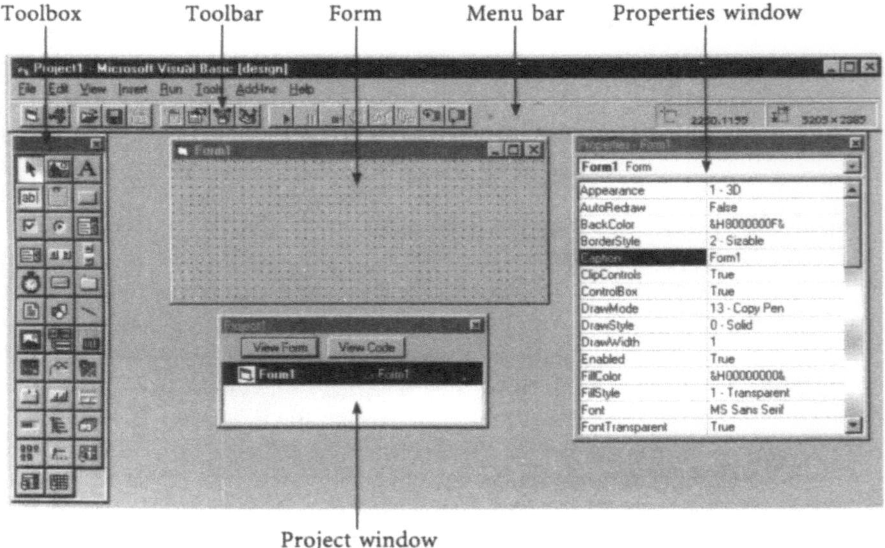

Fig. 1.3 *The Visual Basic design screen.*

The screen has four windows:

- The form, which is where you create the form that you are designing.
- The toolbox with "controls" such as buttons and lists.
- The control properties window.
- The project window.

In addition there is:

- The Visual Basic menu bar and toolbar.

The Form

The main part of the design screen is the form, which will be similar to the one shown in fig. 1.4.

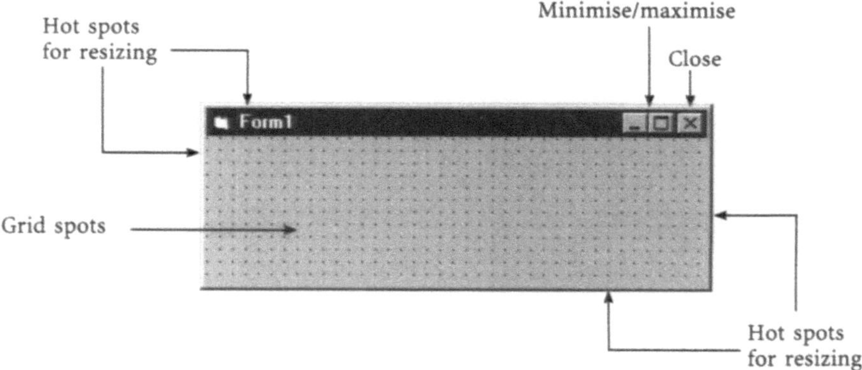

Fig. 1.4   *The design form.*

This has the default heading of *Form1*. If you create a second form it will have the default name of *Form2*, and so on. The naming sequence is logical but not imaginative. If you want to change it you can.

This form has all the usual features of a window. The hot spots are used for resizing the form. When the mouse pointer is on a hot spot, a double-ended arrow is shown. By pressing the left mouse button and dragging, the form border can be moved to shrink or enlarge the form. When the minimise button is pressed, the form is reduced to an icon as shown in fig. 1.5. Double click on it to restore it.

Fig. 1.5   *Minimised forms.*

Every Visual Basic program has at least one form that is used to design the user interface that you want for your program. The toolbox provides the tools to add buttons, text boxes, captions, combo boxes and all the other standard Windows elements that make up the user interface. All of these elements are called "controls".

The grid dots are used to align controls. When you insert a control, such as a button or list, it will "snap" to the nearest grid point. You can alter the spacing of the grid points or disable the grid altogether. Each type of control has a set of configurable properties associated with it.

The Toolbox

The toolbox is used to put the controls, such as buttons, text and menus, on the form. The toolbox contains a number of controls that represent all the Windows objects that you can use when designing your application interface. The toolbox controls are shown in fig. 1.6.

Fig. 1.6
The Toolbox – with and without the custom controls.

The controls are placed on the form by selecting them, that is by clicking on the control. Click on the form in the position on the form where you want the control to be inserted. Next, press the left button again and drag the mouse with the button still pressed. A box appears which defines the area for the control. When you release the left button, the control appears. Both the position and the size of the controls can be altered at any time. Most programmers would position the controls approximately and fine-tune later. The controls in the toolbox are dealt with in chapter 5.

The Control Properties Window

The control properties window lists all the properties of the form. When you add controls to the form a new properties window is created for each control, but only one properties window can be displayed at any time. **Caption** is one of the properties of a form that can be changed to give a more meaningful name than *Form1*.

The Project Window

A project is a collection of files that comprise an application. Every application needs to have a project file. The project window, shown in fig. 1.7, is a text file that lists all the current files in the project.

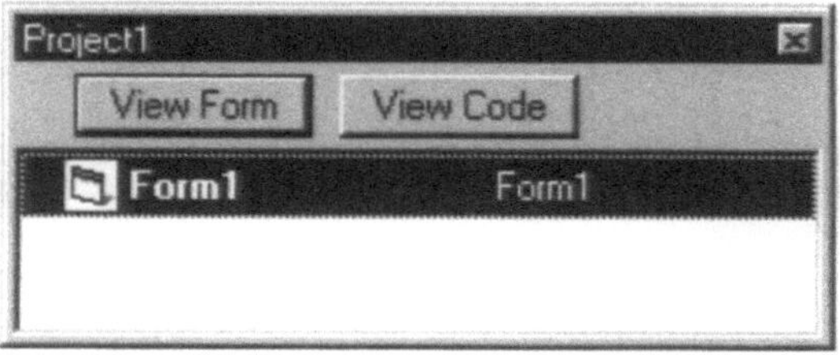

Fig. 1.7
The project window.

The project window provides a quick way to find any file. The project window itself can be found by selecting the **Window** option from the **View** menu which lists all windows that are available.

The Visual Basic Menu Bar and Toolbar

The Visual Basic Menu bar, shown in fig 1.8 is directly under the title bar.

Fig. 1.8   The menu bar.

This is familiar to anyone who has used a Windows program. The options on the Visual Basic menu bar are:

File allows the user to open and save files.

Edit provides editing options such as **Cut** and **Paste** and **Search**.

Visual Basic programs are governed by events on the form. When an event, such as a button click, occurs an associated procedure is called. The procedures are named using a convention based on the name of the control and the type of event that occurs. The **View** option allows the user to step from one procedure to another. If you lose the toolbox or project window, the **View** menu will display it for you.

Insert allows you to add new forms and modules to the application.

The **Run** option starts the program running, restarts it if it is paused during debugging, or stops it.

The **Tools** option allows you to edit watch points. The **Options** option controls key features about the project and run-time environment, such as the first form to be displayed when an application is run.

The **Add-ins** option runs the **Data Manager** and the **Report Designer** which runs the Crystal Report writer for Visual Basic.

The **Help** option provides a comprehensive Help facility.

The toolbar provides a short-cut way of invoking the most common features on the menu bar. All of these are looked at in detail later, but the best way to learn Visual Basic is to write a program.

Event-Driven Software

If you have programmed before in languages such as Pascal or C, you need to think in a different way to program in Visual Basic. When a Windows program runs, the user is usually presented with a screen consisting of a form with a number of controls. The user decides what happens next, perhaps by clicking on a button, selecting a list item or inputting text. Everything the user does is viewed by the application as an event, and the programmer who wrote the application needs to make sure that every event that occurs is dealt with. This is called event-driven software.

In Visual Basic every event has a name and an event procedure associated with it that makes a response to that event. If, for example, you double click on a button, you need to write some Basic code to take some appropriate action. Visual Basic produces template event procedures for events which you want to respond to; the programmer has to supply the detail.

One of the best ways to learn a language is to write a program and to see some of these ideas in action.

Outline of the Add Program

The Add program adds two numbers together. The final user interface will be similar to the one shown in fig. 1.9.

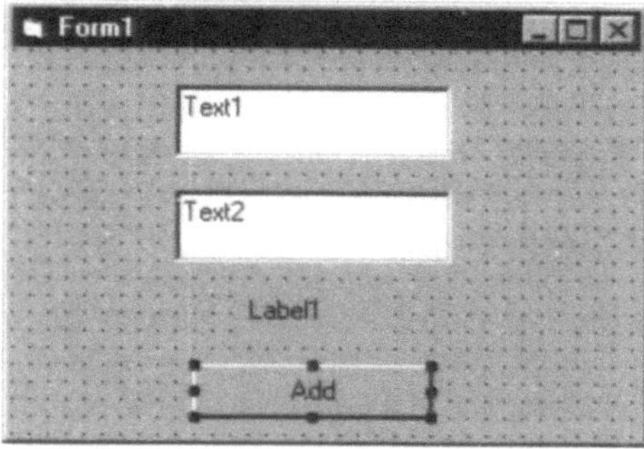

Fig. 1.9
The Add program.

Two numbers are typed into the *Text1* and the *Text2* boxes, and when the button is clicked the numbers are added together and the result displayed into the *Label1* box.

Creating a New Project

The first stage in any program is to create a new project. This is done using the **New Project** option from the **File** menu (fig. 1.10). This creates a form file with an FRM extension and a project file with a VBP extension.

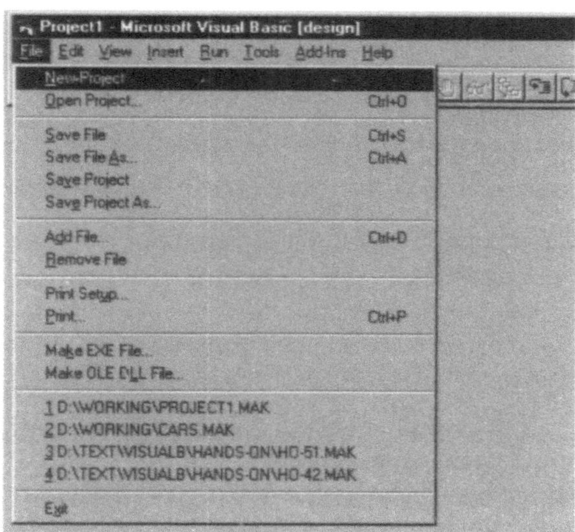

Fig. 1.10
Creating a new project.

Next you need to define the user interface. and write the code to process the input data.

The project can be saved by choosing the **Save Project** option from the **File** menu. You are prompted to supply the name of the form (FRM) file and the name of the Project (VBP) file. The Add program only has two files. One is an FRM file which contains the form, the controls on the form and all the Basic code that deals with the events associated with this form. The second is a project file which contains details of all the forms in this project.

Every Visual Basic project has a project file which is automatically produced when a new project is created. This file contains details such as the first form to be loaded and the name of the required VBX files. Most of the time you can rely on defaults and do not have to change this file.

Defining the User Interface

The window headed *Form1* is where you define your user interface. This is created automatically when you create a new project. The window can be scaled or moved in the usual way for a window, by dragging on one of the handles.

Fig. 1.11   *Adding controls.*

To add the controls to the form (fig. 1.11):

- From the toolbar, click on the TextBox control to select this control.
- Position the cursor on the form.
- Press the left mouse button, and drag to give the size of text box that you want.
- Reposition the cursor and repeat to give the second text box.
- Select the button control and put a button on the screen.
- Select the label control and put the label on the screen.

Moving and Scaling

All the controls on a form can be moved about on that form. Each control can have its size changed, both horizontally and vertically.

Any component can be selected by clicking on it. A group of components can be selected by pressing the left mouse button and dragging. As you do this a rectangle appears. All controls that are completely within the rectangle are selected.

Selected components can be moved by pressing the left mouse button within the selected area, not on one of the handles, and dragging the mouse.

All the control boxes and buttons created can be scaled by clicking on the corner or side handles of a selected control and dragging the handle. This can be done at any stage to enhance the appearance of your user interface.

The Properties Window

When a control is created, a set of default properties are assigned. When a control is selected, its properties are automatically displayed in its **Properties** window (fig. 1.12). By selecting the **Properties** window, the properties of the control can be viewed and modified.

Any changes made in the **Properties** window are immediately reflected in the form being designed.

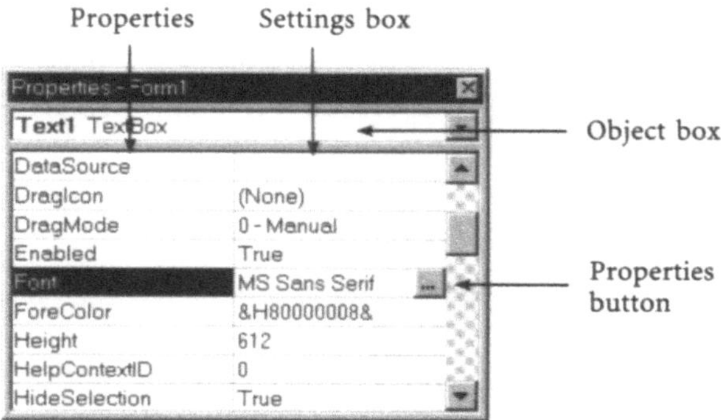

Fig. 1.12   *The **Properties** window.*

- The object box is displayed just under the title bar. This displays the name of the object that currently holds the focus, and what type of object it is.
- In the above example, the object is of type **TextBox** and is called *Text1*.
- The settings box displays the value of the selected property, and allows you to modify it.

If the **Properties** box is inadvertently closed, click on the **View** option from the toolbar and select the option for displaying the properties box. You can use **F4** as a short-cut.

Changing Captions

As you click on any of the boxes or buttons, the **Properties** window changes. This windows box displays the information associated with the selected control. You can move up and down the alphabetical list of properties using the right vertical scroll bar on the right of the window. For this exercise, the caption of the button is changed to **Add** and the captions for the two text boxes are changed to be blank. To change the caption of the **Add** control:

- Select the button control. This will cause the **Properties** window to display the properties of this control.
- Select the **Caption** property (fig. 1.13) and change to **Add**.

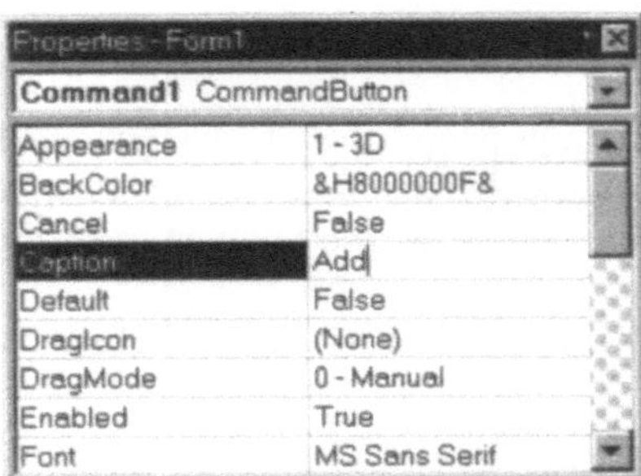

Fig. 1.13
The **Caption** property.

Note: Each of the boxes has a label, which is how Visual Basic refers to that component. You can change the label, but for now use the default labels of *Text1*, *Text2* and *Label1*.

Writing the Code

After designing the form the supporting code has to be written. When you click on a button, this causes a **Click** event. Visual Basic automatically creates the header and terminator for the procedure that processes the button click event:

> ***Private Sub** Command1_Click ( )*
> ***End Sub***

Notice that the procedure name consists of the control name, an underscore and the word Click. This code is displayed in a code window as shown in fig. 1.4.

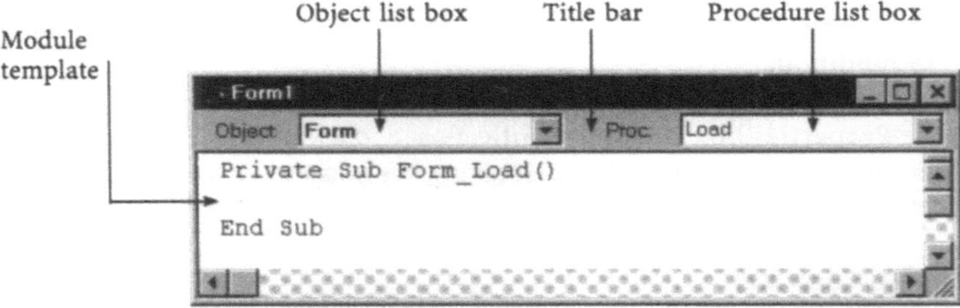

Fig. 1.14   The code window.

Any object in the application can be specified by viewing and selecting the object displayed in the object list box. An object may have many events associated with it, for example, a button may have a click event and a double click event. You can select the event procedure that you want to see by selecting it in the procedure list box.

When an event occurs, the program will execute the event procedure associated with this event. There are three ways to view the outline procedure created by Visual Basic:

- Double click on the **Add** button and Visual Basic displays the associated code.
- Choose the **Code** option from the **View** menu (short-cut key F7).
- Select the form in the Projects window and click on **View Code.**

The code that you need to type in between the **Sub** line and the **End Sub** line is:

Label1 = Val(Text1) + Val(Text2)

- **Val** is a function that converts the text string into a number
- *Text1* and *Text2* are the values of strings which are typed into the two text boxes
- *Label1* is the value of the contents of the label box called *Label1*.

The new value of *Label1* is displayed at the end of the event.

Running the Program

The program is now ready to run (fig. 1.15).

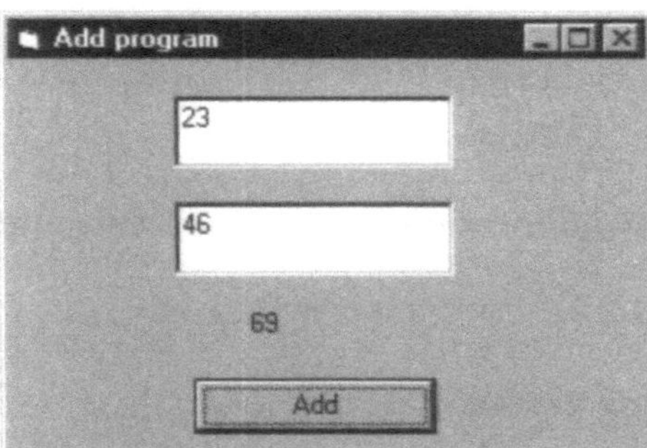

Fig. 1.15
The completed Add program.

This can only be run within the Visual Basic environment. There are two ways to run the program:

- Press the **Run** button on the toolbar (fig. 1.16).
- or select the **Run** menu and choose the **Start** option.

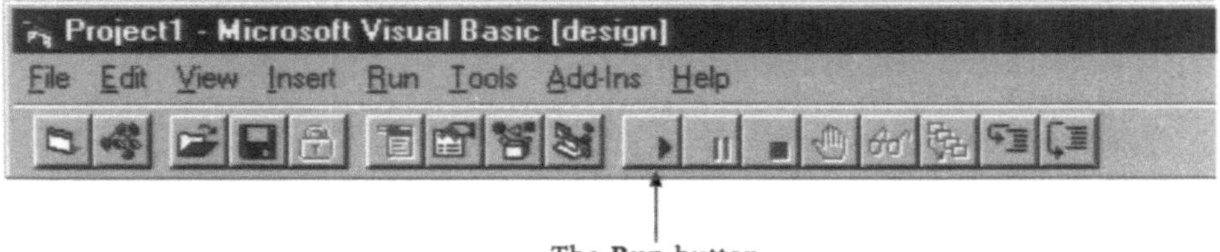

The **Run** button

Fig. 1.16 *Running the completed program.*

If you want to run the program outside the Visual Basic environment, you need to make a Windows executable file. To do this, choose **Make EXE** from the **File** menu. You are asked for a file name for your EXE file: use *Adder*. If you click on **Options**, the dialog box in fig 1.17 is shown.

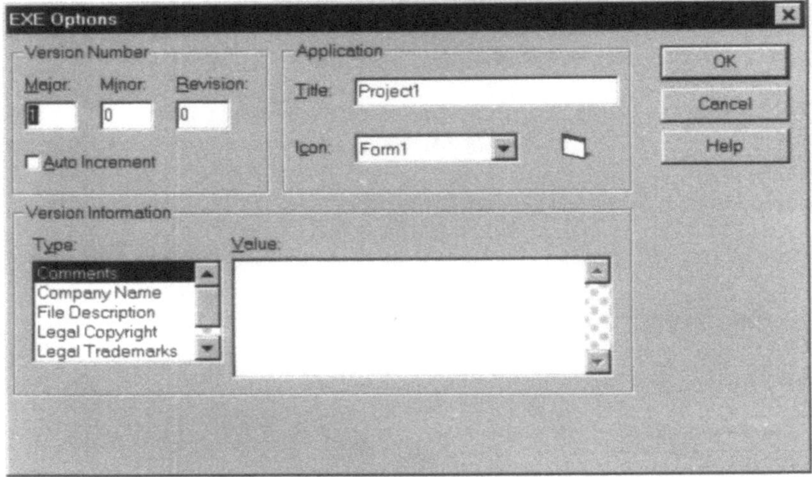

Fig. 1.17 *The EXE options dialog box.*

This dialog box allows you to add information such as the version number and version information.

To run the EXE you have created:

- Click on Start on the Windows 95 taskbar
- Click on **Programs**
- Click on Windows Explorer
- Select **Find** under the **Tools** menu
- Search for the adder.exe file and click on its icon to run it.

Using Properties

You have seen how some properties of some controls can be changed. In fact, all controls and forms have properties that can be seen in the properties window.

The properties can be referred to as:

Controlname.Property

For example:

Text1.BackColor = 0

If your project has more than one form, you may need to refer to a property of other forms from within a form or code module. For example, to refer to the **Caption** property of *Form1*:

*Form1.**Caption** = "This is a new caption"*

To refer to a control's property in another form, the name of the form followed by the "!" operator must be used. For example:

*Form1!Text1.**Text** = "This is new text"*

It is syntactically acceptable to use the "." operator instead of "!" for compatibility with version 1.0 of Visual Basic; however it is not recommended, as "!" provides much greater clarity of exactly what is happening.

Enabled and Name Properties

The **Enabled** and **Name** properties are common to most controls.

- If the **Enabled** property is set to true, the control can respond to any event. If it is set to false, the control does not respond to any event.
- The **Name** property specifies the name of the control.
- When an event procedure for a control is created it needs to know the name of the control. If the name is changed after an event procedure has been created, the event procedure name must be changed manually.
- It is recommended that any changes to controls or forms should be done before any event procedures are created.

Control Values

All controls have a property that is used for storing the value of that control:

- For example, for text boxes, this property is **Text**.
- If a text box is called *Text1*, the **Text** property of this box is called *Text1.**Text***; however, this can be referred to as *Text1*.

*Text1.**Text** = "hello"*

and

Text1 = "hello"

Both of these perform the same operation, but the second version generates a slightly more efficient run-time code, although it is less readable.

The most common controls and the properties that are their values are shown in the table.

Control	Property
CheckBox	Value
ComboBox	Text
CommandButton	Value
DirListBox	Path
DriveListBox	Drive
FileListBox	FileName
Frame	Caption
HScrollBar	Value
Label	Caption
Line	Visible
ListBox	Text
Menu	Enabled
OptionButton	Value
Picture	Picture
TextBox	Text
Timer	Enabled
VScrollBar	Value

Controlling Form Properties

In the Add program, the **Caption** was changed. In addition, many other features of the form can be controlled by first selecting the form and then changing the properties in the properties window. The most common properties that are changed for a form are:

- The **BorderStyle** property, which has four possible settings.

Property Value	Effect
0	The form has no border.
1	The border has minimise and maximise buttons and a control box. It has no hot spots and the window cannot be resized or moved.
2	The default. The border has minimise and maximise buttons, a control box and hot spot. It is resizable.
3	The border has a control box.

- If **MinButton** is set to true, the form has a minimise button.
- If **MaxButton** is set, the form has a maximise button.
- If the **BorderStyle** property is either 0 or 3, these properties have no effect.

- The **BackColor** property controls the background colour of the form. In order to see the colours available, select this property and click on the row of dots (fig. 1.18).

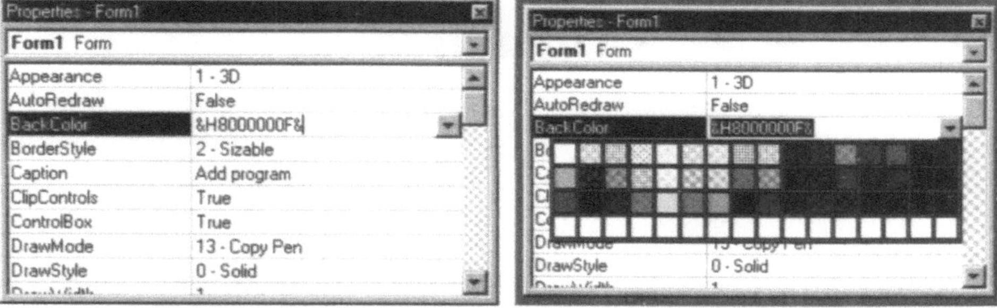

Fig. 1.18 The **BackColor** property.

2

How Projects are Organised

Introduction

When you are creating an application in Visual Basic, all the necessary files are grouped together in a project. The first stage in developing an application is to create a new project. In this chapter you will learn about:

- Project elements.
- Creating forms.
- Creating and saving modules.

The File Menu

The **File** menu is used for creating and saving forms, files and projects. The options available under the **File** Menu used for this are:

Menu Command	Description
New Project	Starts a new project after prompting the user to save the current project. When you run Visual Basic, a new project is automatically started.
Open Project	Loads an existing project after prompting to save the current project.
Save Project	Saves all files associated with the current project.
Save Project As	Saves all existing project files and prompts the user for a project name.

When a project is being saved, the project (VBP) file is saved last, since this contains the location of all the project files. Modification of this file is not recommended.

Application Files

The different aspects of an application are described in a collection of files. These files are used to build the application.

Projects consist of the following:

- One file for each form (FRM).
- One file for each code module (BAS).
- One file for each custom component (VBX or OCX).
- One project file which keeps a track of all the other components (VBP).
- One file per form, if required, to store an associated binary data item (FRX).
- A resource file (RES).
- A CLS file for each class module.

The files in the project are combined to form a single executable Windows application (EXE).

The project window is a text file that lists all the current files in the project.

FRM Files

Forms have an FRM extension. They contain:

- A full graphical description of the form.
- The controls on the form.
- The event procedures.
- Sometimes general procedures, although these are more usually contained in a BAS file.

Applications can have multiple forms, but each form is saved as a separate file. Forms are managed by three commands on the **Insert** menu:

Menu Command	Description
Form	Creates a new form and adds it to the project.
MDI Form	Creates a new MDI form and adds it to the project.
Module	Creates a new module and adds it to the project.

BAS Files

BAS files are modules that contain:

- Code that is independent of any form.
- General procedures, not event-driven procedures.

- Global and module declarations of types, constants and variables.

To create a new BAS file use the **Module** option from the **Insert** menu.
To add an existing module, use the **Add File** option from the **File** menu.

VBX and OCX Files

Custom controls are built in Visual Basic and have a VBX or an OCX extension. They include:

- The Grid control
- The **CommonDialog** control
- The OLE (Object Linking and Embedding) control.

Many third parties are selling a wide range of VBX files. If you want to see the custom controls that you have installed – or wish to install another – choose the **Custom Controls** option from the **Tools** menu as shown in fig. 2.1.

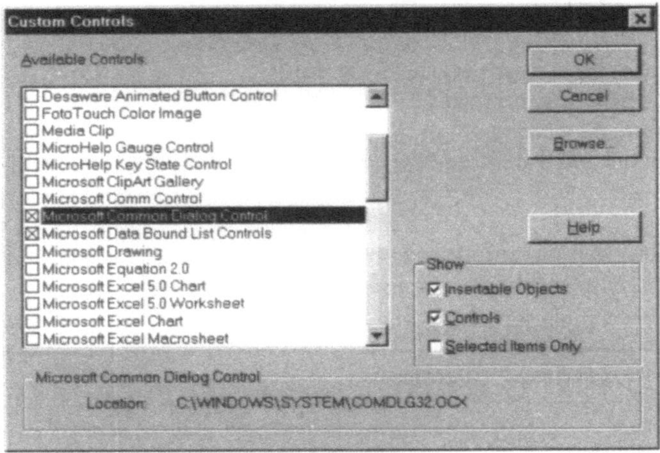

Fig. 2.1   *The **CommonDialog** controls.*

The OCX files are OLE custom controls. They are similar to the VBX files except that VBX files can only be used with 16-bit versions of Visual Basic, while OCX files can be used in both 16- and 32-bit applications. It is advisable to replace your VBX controls from earlier versions of Visual Basic with OCX files. To do this choose **Options** from the **Tools** menu and click on the **Advanced** page tab (fig. 2.2).

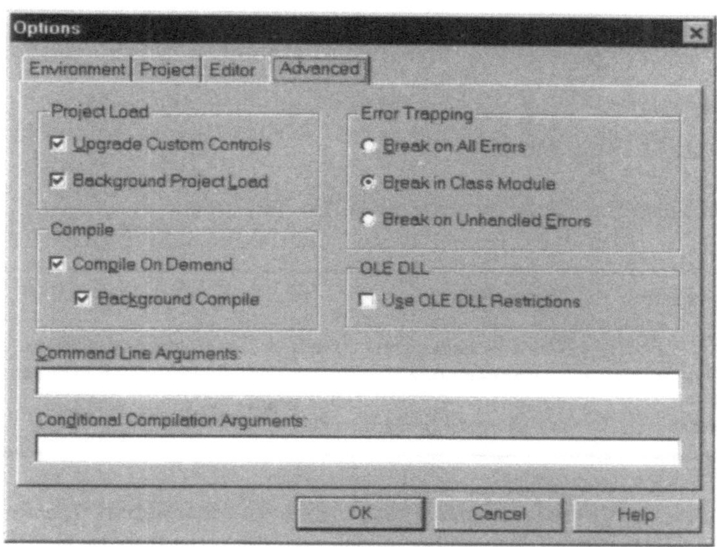

Fig. 2.2   *Updating VBX controls with OCX controls.*

When you load a project that uses VBX files, you will be prompted to replace the VBX controls with OCX controls where there is an equivalent control, as shown in fig. 2.3.

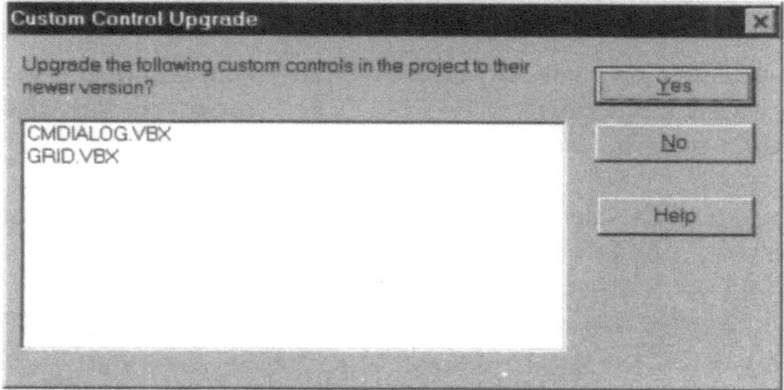

Fig. 2.3   *Custom control upgrade.*

FRX Files

FRX files are used for storing binary data:

- For example, picture boxes have a **Picture** property. The binary picture is stored in an FRX file.

- There is one FRX file at most per form.
- FRX files are managed by Visual Basic without user intervention.
- FRX files have the same name as the associated form.

Creating and Saving Modules

Files are managed by four commands on the **File** menu:

Menu Command	Description
Add File	Adds an existing form, module or custom control to a project.
Remove File	Removes an existing form, module or custom control from a project.
Save File	Saves a form or module in a project.
Save File As	Saves a form or module under a specified name.

If you remove a file from a project, the project file is updated. If a file is deleted outside of Visual Basic, this may cause problems as the project file will be incorrect. It makes sense to deal with all changes to the files in a project by using the Visual Basic menu system.

It is important to note that if a file is added to a project, a copy of it is not made – there is simply a reference to it in the project file, so any file, form or module can be a part of more than one project.

The Autoload File

The autoload file is automatically added to the project file when you create a new application. This file is called AUTO32LD.VBP. To edit this file, select the **Open Project** option from the **File** menu and choose that file name.

- To remove a file, select it in the projects window and choose the **Remove File** option from the **File** menu.
- To add a file, choose the **Add File** option from the **File** menu.
- To change the custom controls, choose **Custom Controls** from the **Tools** menu.
- When you have made all the required changes, choose **Save Project** from the **File** menu.

3

The Toolbar and Menu

Introduction

In this chapter you will learn about:

- The toolbar and the menu.

The Toolbar

The toolbar (fig. 3.1) provides a short-cut way of invoking frequently needed functions without the need to go through the menu bar.

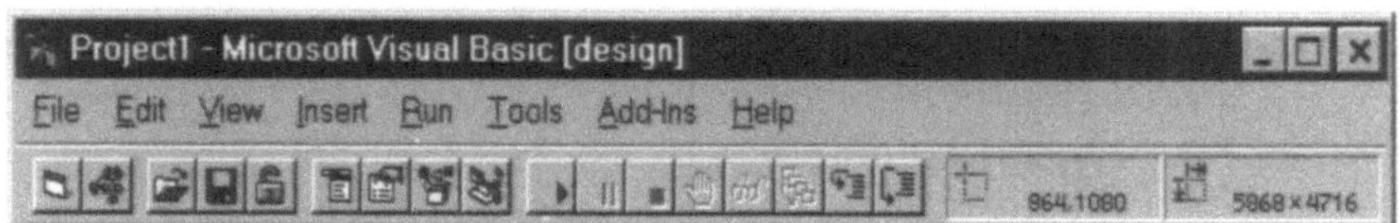

Fig. 3.1 *The toolbar.*

The toolbar contains four groups of buttons which are used for:

- Adding new forms or modules.
- Opening and saving files and projects.
- Displaying Windows.
- Controlling the running and debugging of the program.

The toolbar buttons are:

Project and File Management

Button	Function	Equivalent Menu Command
	Creates a new form	**Form** on the **Insert** menu
	Creates a new module	**Module – Insert** menu
	Opens an existing project	**Open Project – File** menu
	Saves the current project	**Save Project – File** menu
	Locks and unlocks controls on the currently active form	**Lock Controls – Edit** menu

Displaying Windows

Button	Function	Equivalent Menu Command
	Displays the menu editor	**Menu Editor – Tools** menu
	Displays the properties window	**Properties – View** menu
	Displays the object browser	**Object Browser – View** menu
	Displays the projects window	**Project – View** menu

Running and Debugging Applications

Button	Function	Equivalent Menu Command
	Starts an application in design mode	**Start – Run** menu
	Stops execution of a running program	**Break – Run** menu
	Stops application of an application and returns to the **Design** menu	**End command – Run** menu
	Toggles the breakpoint on the current line	**Toggle breakpoint – Run** menu

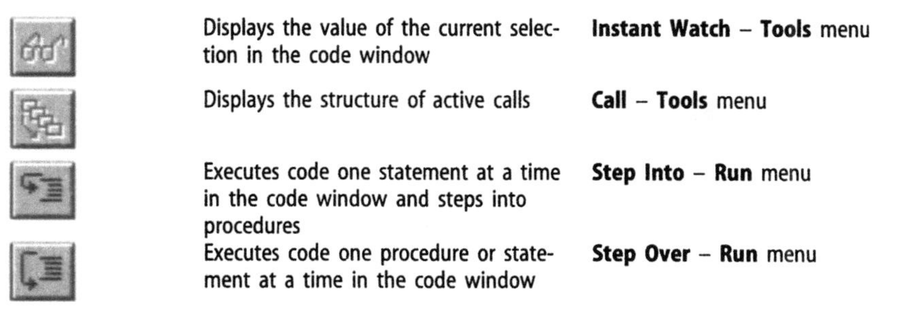

	Displays the value of the current selection in the code window	**Instant Watch** – **Tools** menu
	Displays the structure of active calls	**Call** – **Tools** menu
	Executes code one statement at a time in the code window and steps into procedures	**Step Into** – **Run** menu
	Executes code one procedure or statement at a time in the code window	**Step Over** – **Run** menu

The Menu

Visual Basic provides excellent help facilities. There are two ways of getting help:

- Select **Help** from the menu bar. One of the most effective ways of obtaining help is to select the **Search** facility of the **Help** utility which is found on the menu bar.

Or

- Move the mouse to the item you want help on and press F1. The advantage of using **F1** is that it provides context-sensitive help.

The **Help** facility is very similar to that found in most Windows products and is fairly intuitive to use.

The Print Dialog Box

The **File** menu is also used for printing. The **Print** option in this menu offers several choices in the **Print** dialog box (fig. 3.2).

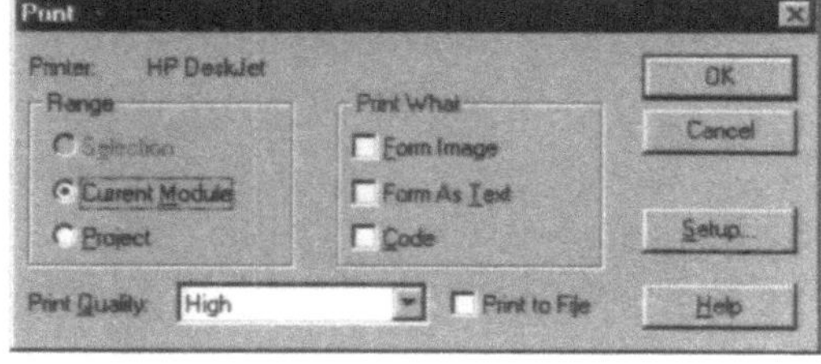

Fig. 3.2
The **Print** dialog box.

The **Range** options control the range that you print:

- **Selection** – prints the currently selected code.
- **Current Module** – prints the forms and code for the selected module.
- **Project** – prints the forms and code for the whole project.

The **Print What** options determine what you can print.

- Form Image – print an image of the form.
- Forms as Text – prints the textual representation of the form.
- Code – prints code.

The Edit Menu

Visual Basic has an editor which is very similar to that found in many Windows applications:

Menu Command	Description
Undo	Undoes the previous editing action. You can undo up to 20 previous actions. **Ctrl+Z** is the short-cut.
Redo	Does the previous undo action. **Ctrl+Backspace** is the short-cut.
Cut	Removes selected text and places it in the clipboard. **Ctrl+X** is the short-cut.
Copy	Places selected text into the clipboard but does not delete it. **Ctrl+C** is the short-cut.
Paste	Inserts the contents of the clipboard. **Ctrl+V** is the short-cut.
Delete	Deletes the selected text. The **Del** key can be used instead.

Finding and Replacing Text

The **Find** option is used for searching through modules of the entire project for text and replacing it as necessary. The **Find** dialog box is shown in fig. 3.3.

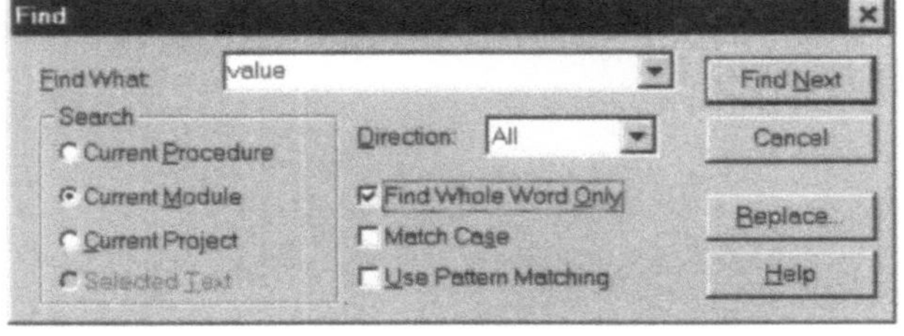

Fig. 3.3
The **Find** dialog box.

The **Search** options determine what is searched – the current procedure, module or Project or selected text.

You can specify that you are searching for the whole word; for example, if you are searching for an identifier called *val*, if the **Find Whole Word Only** box is checked it will ignore identifiers such as *val1* and *value*. You can use pattern-matching characters so that, for example, *c?t* will find *cat* and *cot*.

Image Priority

Visual Basic can display a variety of controls which may overlap. By specifying the image priority, the way in which objects overlap can be controlled.

Menu Command	Description
Bring to Front	Brings a selected object to the foreground. The short-cut is **Ctrl + =**.
Send to Back	Moves a selected object to the background behind all other objects. The shortcut is **Ctrl + -**.
Align to Grid	Moves the selected controls to align with the nearest grid points.
Lock	Locks all the controls on a form in their current position so that you cannot move them. This applies to the current form.

The **Align to Grid** option is only needed if the automatic align to grid has been explicitly removed by using **the Environment** page of the **Options** option in the **Tools** menu.

The Tools Menu

The **Options** option from the **Tools** menu has four pages which control details about the development environment and project.

The **Environment** page controls a range of settings concerning the presentation and use of the Visual Basic desktop, as shown in fig. 3.4.

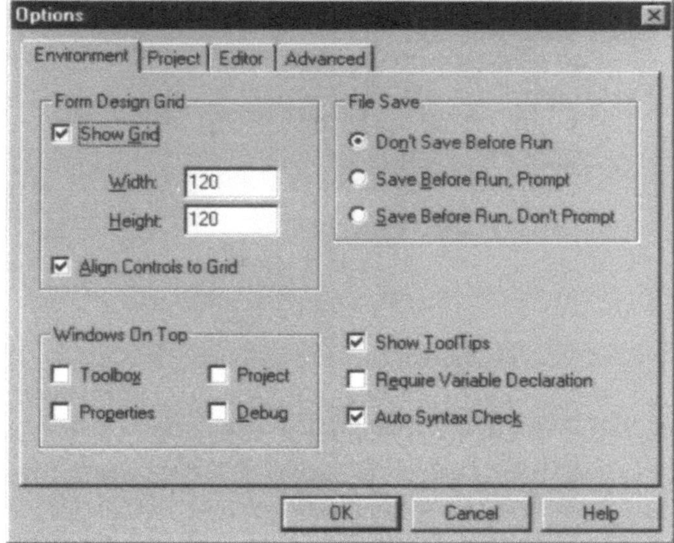

Fig. 3.4 *The* **Environment** *page.*

The **Form Design Grid** options controls how the grid on the design forms appears at design-time; the grid will not be seen at run-time:

- **Show Grid** – makes the grid visible or invisible.
- **Width, Height** – the width and height of grid cells from 45 to 1485 twips.
- **Align Components to Grid** – ensures that the outer edges of components are aligned with the grid.

Windows On Top options – any of the checked windows will remain at the front when displayed.

Require Variable Declaration option allows you to make the declaration of variables before their use mandatory. It is recommended that you use this option to avoid programming errors. It has the same effect as adding the **Option Explicit** directive to the general declarations section of new modules.

Auto Syntax Check option determines whether Visual Basic immediately checks the syntax of every line after it has been typed.

Save Before Run determines whether you are prompted to save all files before running an application.

The main items on the **Project** page, shown in fig. 3.5, are:

- **Startup Form** – this is the name of the first form to be displayed when the application runs.
- **Help File** – the name of a help file that is available to your application.
- The **StartMode** option determines if the application is standalone or started as part of an OLE application.

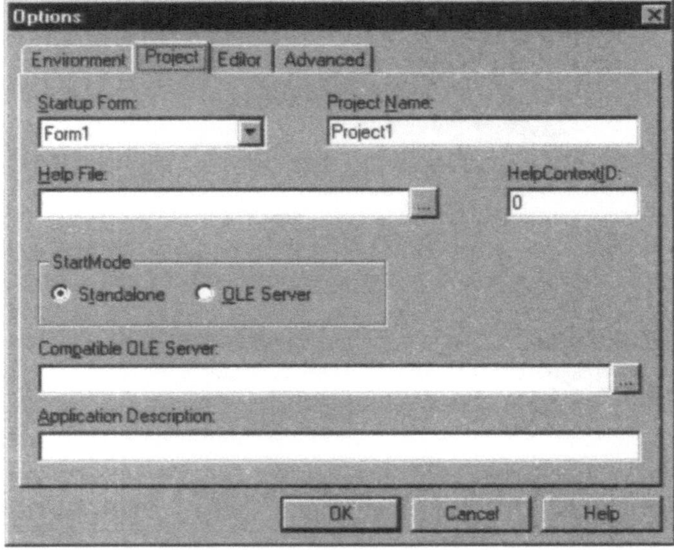

Fig. 3.5   The **Project** page.

The **Editor** page, shown in fig. 3.6, allows you to specify the appearance of the text in your development environment if you do not like the default set of options.

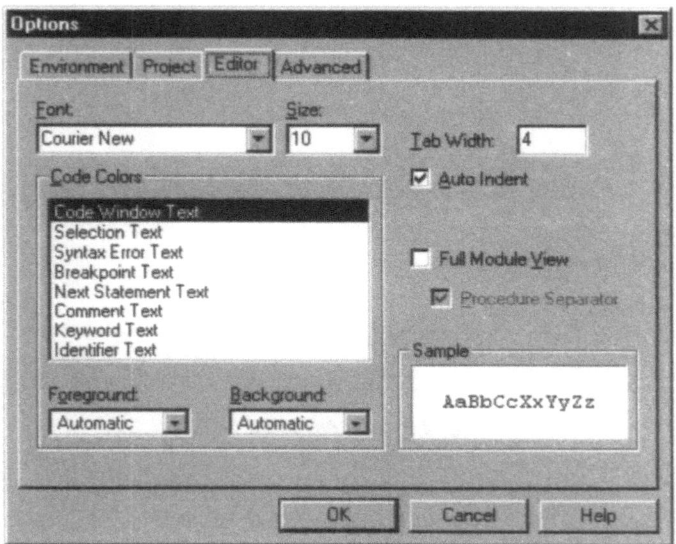

Fig. 3.6   *The **Editor** page.*

The **Advanced** page, shown in fig. 3.7, controls the following settings.
The **Project Load** options:

- **Upgrade Custom Controls** – if this option is selected, Visual Basic will upgrade all the VBX controls in a project when it loads, and will replace each control with an OLE custom (OCX) file if one is available.
- **Background Project Load** – determines if code is loaded in the background.

The **Compile** options:

- **Compile on Demand** – if checked and a project has changed, it will not be recompiled before being run.
- **Background Compile** – determines if idle time is used during run-time to finish compiling the application in the background. Selecting this option can improve run-time execution speed. It is not active unless the **Compile on Demand** option is also checked.

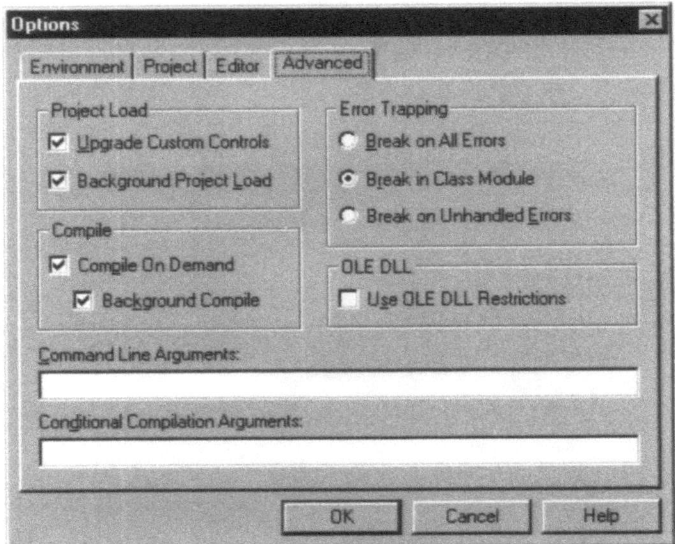

Fig. 3.7   *The **Advanced** page.*

The **Error Trapping** options controls how Visual Basic handles errors:

- **Break on All Errors** – any error transfers controls to break mode, whether an error handler is active or not.
- **Break in Class Module** – any errors that occur in a class module and are not handled cause the project to enter break mode.
- **Break on Unhandled Errors** – if an error occurs and an error handler is active, the error is trapped without going into break mode.

The View Menu

This menu option allows you to select a window to be displayed. An annoying problem when developing Visual Basic applications is that so many Windows are needed.

- The **Code** option displays the code window for the current form or module.
- The **Form** option displays the currently selected form module.
- The **Project** option displays the project window.
- The **Properties** option displays the properties window for the currently selected control.
- The **Toolbox** and **Toolbar** options display these windows.
- The **Color Palette** option displays the dialog box shown in fig. 3.8.

Fig. 3.8 *The color palette.*

This control allows you to change the colours and background of a form. It is only available at design-time.

4

General Procedures and DLLS

Introduction

A procedure is a collection of program statements that behave as a unit. In Visual Basic the procedures that deal with the events that happen, such as buttons being clicked or text being typed, are called event procedures. All other procedures are called general procedures. Procedures are defined as either **SUB** or **FUNCTION**, which behave in slightly different ways. In this chapter you will learn about:

- Event and general procedures.
- **SUB** procedures.
- **FUNCTION** procedures.
- Naming conventions.
- How to declare DLLs.
- How to call DLLs.

General Procedures

A procedure that is not invoked in response to an event is called a general procedure.

- Events often cause similar operations to be performed. A single general procedure could be called by a variety of event procedures – so avoiding duplication of code.
- If a general procedure is defined in a form module, it can be called by any of the event procedures in that form.
- If a general procedure is to be called from anywhere in the application it must be in a code module, that is a BAS file.

Event Procedures

When an event occurs in Visual Basic, for example, a button clicking, an event procedure with a name corresponding to the button and the event is invoked. Visual Basic automatically creates a template event procedure with the appropriate name according to the control name and the event type.

The form of event procedures is:

> **Private Sub** *controlname_eventname( )*
>   *statement block*
> **End Sub**

An event procedure name comprises:

- The control's name
- An underscore
- The event name.

For example, if a command button is called *NewButton* and a mouse button is clicked on that button, then a **Click** event occurs and the event procedure is called *NewButton_Click*.

Note: It is the **Name** property of a control that is used in naming the procedures, not the **Caption** property that is displayed on the design screen.

If you change the **Name** property of your controls before writing event procedures for them, the event procedures automatically have the correct name. This is not the case if you change the name afterwards – you have to change the name of the event procedures manually.

Note: Event procedures are always **Sub** procedures, not **Function** procedures. **Sub** procedures do not return a value.

The Scope of Event and General Procedures

All executable code is either in a general procedure or an event procedure.

- Each event procedure is associated with a particular form.
- The same application can have many event procedures with the same name – but associated with different forms. For example, an application may have two forms, each of which has a button called *Button1* with a button click event called *Button1_Click*. When a click occurs, the event procedure connected to the current form is executed.

General procedures can be defined in either the general section of either a form or a code module.

- A general procedure defined in a form can only be called from within that form.
- A general procedure defined in the general section of a code module can be called from anywhere within the application.

Using Event Procedures

In order to write an event procedure for a form or control:

- Double click on the selected object.

This opens the code window.

The code window, shown in fig. 4.1, can also be opened by selecting the **Code** option from the **View** menu, or by pressing the short-cut key **F7**.

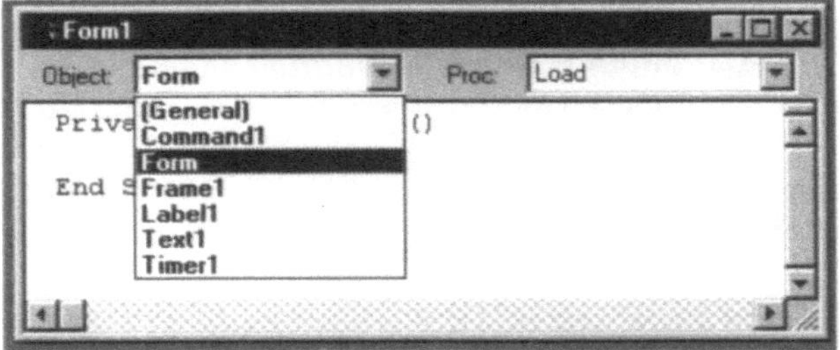

Fig. 4.1
Finding forms.

The object box contains the name of all the objects in the projects. In this case there are general procedures, a command button labelled *Command1* and a form object.

The procedure box lists all the event procedures for the selected object (fig. 4.2).

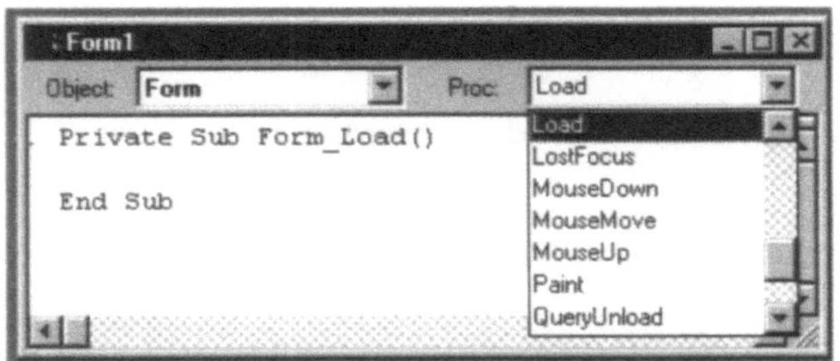

Fig. 4.2
Listing event procedures.

If a new event procedure is selected, a template is created for that event.

Making a New General Procedure

To make a new general procedure:

- Make a code window active.
- Choose **Procedure** from the **Insert** menu.
- Choose either **Sub** or **Function** as the function type.
- Specify the function or procedure name.

A general procedure template similar to one of the two templates shown below is created:

> *Private Sub MyNewProcedure ( )*
>
> *End Sub*
>
> *Private Function MyNewFunction ( )*
>
> *End Function*

Passing Arguments

The syntax for a **Sub** procedure is:

> *Private Sub ProcedureName (argument_list)*
>   *statements*
> *End Sub*

The argument list is a list of argument names separated by commas:

> *[ByVal] variablename [( )] [As type]*

- The **ByVal** keyword indicates that the parameter is being passed by value, not by reference.
- The type specifier gives the type of the variable being passed.

The procedure shown below is called *MyProcedure* and passes two values called *Count* which is an **Integer**, and *Salary*, which is of type **Single**.

> *Private Sub MyProcedure (Count **As Integer**, **ByVal** Salary **As Single**)*

This can be called in two ways, for example, by the statement:

> *MyProcedure 7,50000*

An optional **Call** keyword could be inserted to give:

> *Call MyProcedure (7,50000)*

Function Procedures

The syntax for a **Function** procedure is:

> *Function ProcedureName (argument_list) [As type]*
> > *Statements*
> *End Function*

This operates in exactly the same way as the **Sub** procedure, except for three differences:

- Brackets must always be used around the arguments – **Call** cannot be used.
- Function procedures have data types, just as variables do. This controls the type of return value.
- A value is returned by assigning the function name itself.

A user-defined function procedure can be used in the same way as any of the built-in Visual Basic functions. For example:

> *Function TimesTwo (A) **As Single***
> > *TimesTwo = A * 2*
> *End Function*

This can be called, for example, by the statement:

> *Solution = TimesTwo (7.5)*

Naming Conventions

The names of procedures, variables and constants conform to the same naming rules:

- They must begin with a letter.
- They must contain only letters, numbers and the underscore characters.
- They must be 40 characters or less.
- The names declared in code cannot be the same as reserved words such as **Call** or **Sub**.

DLLs

Dynamic Link Libraries (DLLs) are a key feature of Windows. They are libraries of procedures to which applications can link to at run-time rather than at link time. Visual Basic applications can call the procedures in DLLs to perform actions that cannot be performed directly by Visual Basic.

Using DLLs

DLLs can be updated independently of the applications and more than one application can share the same DLL. DLL procedures are external to your Visual Basic application, therefore, you need to inform your applications of where the DLL is.

There are two stages to using a DLL:

- Use the **Declare** statement to tell Visual Basic where the DLL is.
- Make the actual call to the procedure.

Only one declaration is needed, irrespective of how many times the procedure is called.

Declaring a DLL

- Place a **Declare** statement in the declaration section of a form or code module.
- If you declare the DLL in a form, the DLL is **Private** to that form.
- If you declare it in a code module, it is **Public** and can be called from anywhere in your application.
- If the procedure does not return a value, declare it as a **Sub** procedure.

For example, to declare a DLL:

Declare Sub *CalcArea* **Lib** *"User"* **(ByVal X As Integer)**

If the procedure does return a value, declare it as a Function procedure.

Declare Function *CalcArea* **Lib** *"User"* **(ByVal X As Integer)**

- The library that is used is indicated by the name following the **Lib** keyword.
- For the operating system DLLs, this is either "User", "GDI", "Kernel" and so on.
- For other non-operating system DLLs, a file specification including a path should be used.
- The DLL has a standard extension of DLL.
- By default, Visual Basic passes all arguments by reference; however, many DLLs expect an argument value to be passed. Therefore the keyword **ByVal** must be used before the variable declaration.

Calling a DLL

- When they have been declared, a DLL procedure call is called in exactly the same way as for any Visual Basic procedure.
- As Visual Basic cannot check that the type of parameters passed is correct, this is a potential source of error at run-time.

5
Controls

Introduction

The working components of a form are the controls; these include buttons, list boxes, labels, scroll bars and many others. These controls are found in the toolbox. In this chapter you will learn about:

- The toolbox.
- Labels.
- Text boxes.
- Captions and hot keys.
- Text boxes and passwords.
- Frames.
- Check boxes.
- Option buttons.
- Scroll bars.
- List boxes.
- Combo boxes.
- Custom controls.

All the controls covered in this chapter are those available in the standard version of Visual Basic, apart from the custom controls. Most of the controls that are not covered in this section are described later in the book.

The Toolbox Appearance

The toolbox allows you to select a wide range of controls (fig. 5.1) that can be used to provide the Windows user interface. Most are intuitive to operate, particularly if you are already using Windows programs.

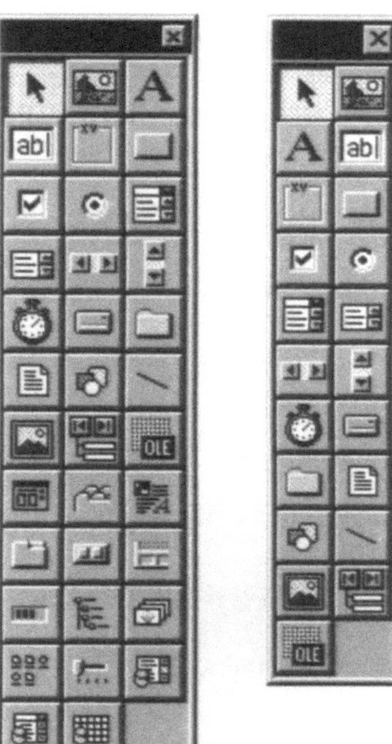

Fig. 5.1
*The toolbox – with and without the custom **controls**.*

Common Toolbox Controls

 **Pointer.** This does not draw a control, but is used to move an existing control.

 **PictureBox.** This control displays graphical images and acts as a container for graphics methods.

 **Label.** Holds text that does not change.

 **TextBox.** Holds text that the user can enter and change.

 **Frame.** Groups controls together, such as options buttons.

 **CommandButton.** A button that can be activated by the user.

 **CheckBox.** A true/false box.

 **OptionButton.** This is used with other options buttons to display a range of choices, only one of which may be selected.

 **ComboBox.** A combination ListBox and TextBox. An item from the list can be selected or text entered.

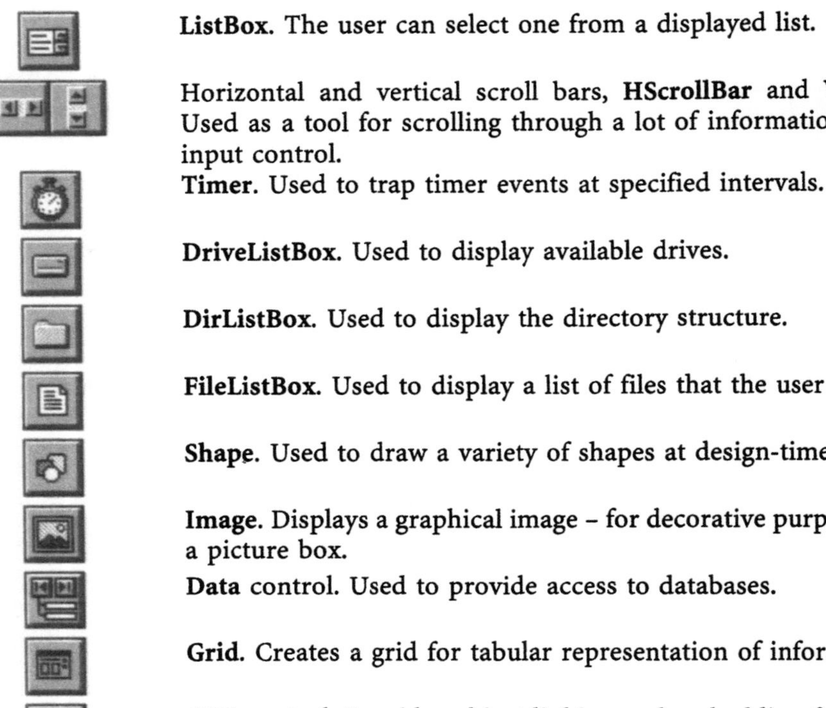

ListBox. The user can select one from a displayed list.

Horizontal and vertical scroll bars, **HScrollBar** and **VScrollBar**. Used as a tool for scrolling through a lot of information, or as an input control.
Timer. Used to trap timer events at specified intervals.

DriveListBox. Used to display available drives.

DirListBox. Used to display the directory structure.

FileListBox. Used to display a list of files that the user can access.

Shape. Used to draw a variety of shapes at design-time.

Image. Displays a graphical image – for decorative purposes, unlike a picture box.
Data control. Used to provide access to databases.

Grid. Creates a grid for tabular representation of information.

OLE control. Provides object linking and embedding from an OLE server into your application.
CommonDialog. Used to create types of dialog boxes for opening and saving files and for setting fonts and colours.

Command Buttons

Each of the controls in the user interface has a property box associated with it. Most are fairly intuitive; however, it is worthwhile reviewing a few key properties. To create a command button, click on the control shown in fig. 5.2.

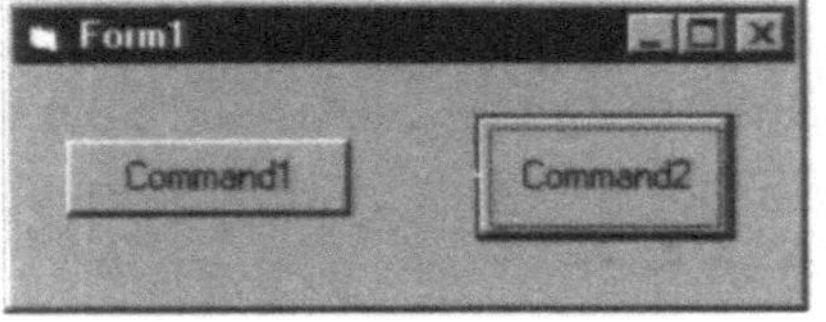

Fig. 5.2 *Creating a **Command** button.*

- The first button has the caption *Command1*, the second *Command2* and so on.

- This can be changed by altering the **Caption** property in the associated properties box.

Labels

Labels (fig. 5.3) can be used to display:

- A small amount of text
- The result of a simple calculation as shown in the *Adder* program
- The first label is called *Label1*, the second *Label2*, and so on.

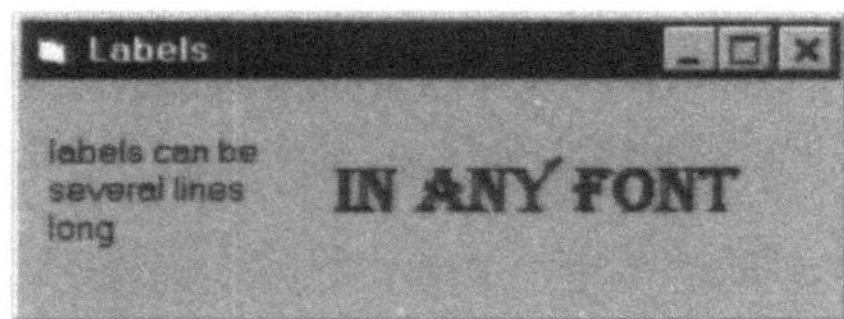

Fig. 5.3 *Creating a **Label** control.*

Text Boxes

Text boxes (fig. 5.4) are used for:

- Displaying or entering a lot of text – up to 32,000 characters.
- The first text box is called *Text1*.

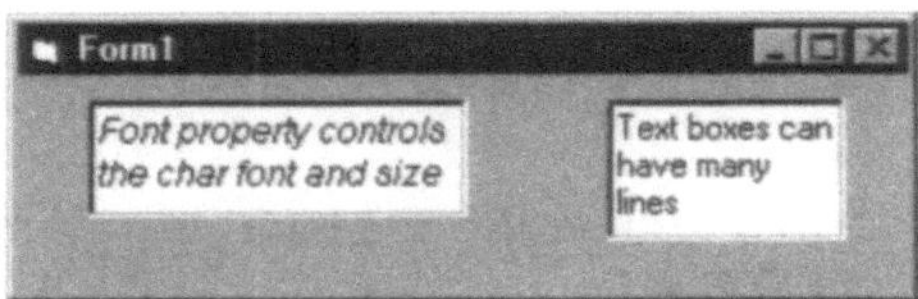

Fig. 5.4 *Creating a **TextBox** control.*

The user can also cut, paste and copy text in a text box, unless the **Enabled** property is set to false.

The contents of the text box are determined by the **Text** property. The format of the text box can also be controlled by, for example, the **BorderStyle** and **ScrollBars** properties (fig. 5.5).

Fig. 5.5 *The **BorderStyle** and **ScrollBars** properties.*

Note: The **MultiLine** property of the text box must be set to true for the **ScrollBars** property to be enabled.

Text Boxes and Passwords

A useful feature of text boxes is that they can be used to input passwords:

- The application designer can set the **Password Char** property to any character, for example, "*".
- When the user types text into this box, each key depression is reflected by this character being displayed in the text box.
- The actual text typed is available for your program to use.

Captions and Hot Keys

Captions are used to identify controls. You can use the default captions or choose your own. You can also use the **Captions** property to create "hot keys".

- For example, if you have a button with a caption of **Quit** and you want **Alt+Q** to be equivalent to pressing this button, set the caption to **&Quit**.
- The "&" character means that **Alt** in conjunction with the following letter can be used to invoke this command.

Frames

The **Frame** control (fig. 5.6) is used to group together sets of controls, for example, to group a set of option buttons.

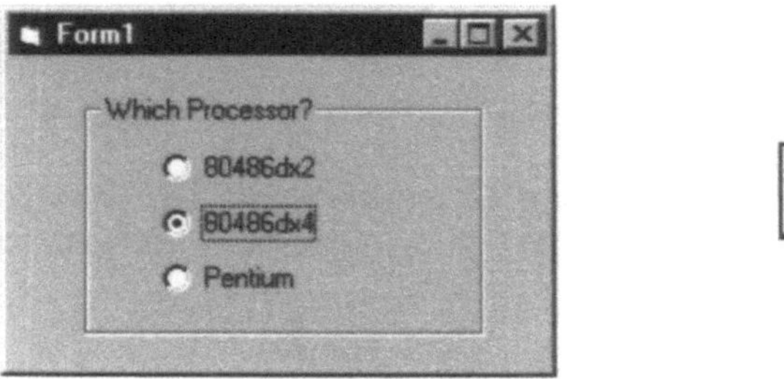

Fig. 5.6   *The **Frame** control.*

- It is important to create the frame first and then add controls to it.
- The first frame is called *Frame1*.

A frame alters the properties of the **Option** buttons that it surrounds and only allows one of a set of **Option** buttons in a frame to be selected. The frame should be created first and then the **Option** buttons placed within it.

Check Boxes

Check boxes (fig. 5.7) are used when the user must specify either a true/false or yes/no answer.

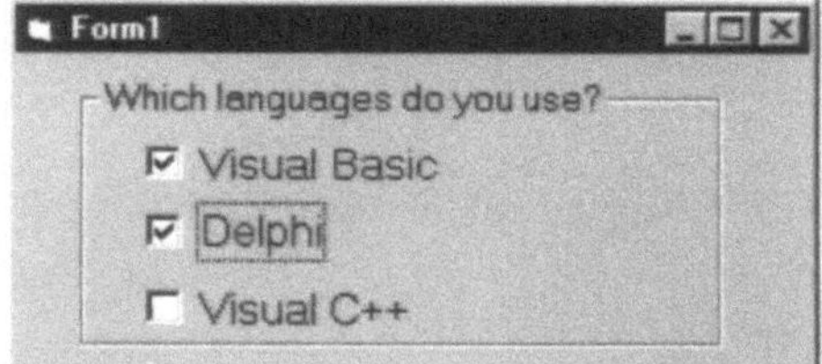

Fig. 5.7 *The **CheckBox** control.*

- The caption of the first box is *Check1* and so on.

Check boxes have a **Value** property.

Value	Description
0	The check box is deselected.
1	The check box is selected.
2	The check box is in an intermediate state.

A check box is displayed as a small square, which, if selected, has a cross in it. If it is not selected, it is blank. Check boxes can also have a grey value, but this must be set under the control of your application program. They have an associated caption as one of their features. In fig. 5.7 the caption is *which language do you use?* A label control is not necessary.

Option Buttons

Option buttons are in some ways similar to check boxes.

- Option buttons always appear in groups and only one of the group can be selected at a time.

- The first option button is called *Option1*.

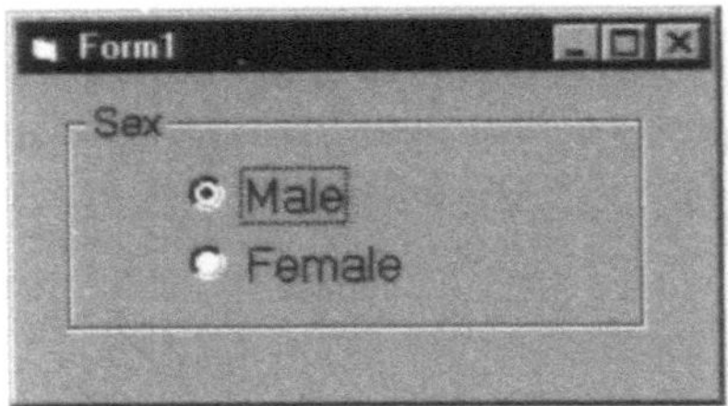

Fig. 5.8   The **OptionButton** control.

An option button includes a caption and so it is not necessary to add a label to explain what the button is for. This differs from a text box which is often accompanied by a label box to explain its purpose. A group of option buttons are shown in fig. 5.8.
Note: You need to group option buttons together using the frame control.

Scroll Bars

Scroll bars (fig. 5.9) are a useful form of user interface, for example, in word processors for moving through the document. There are two forms – vertical and horizontal.

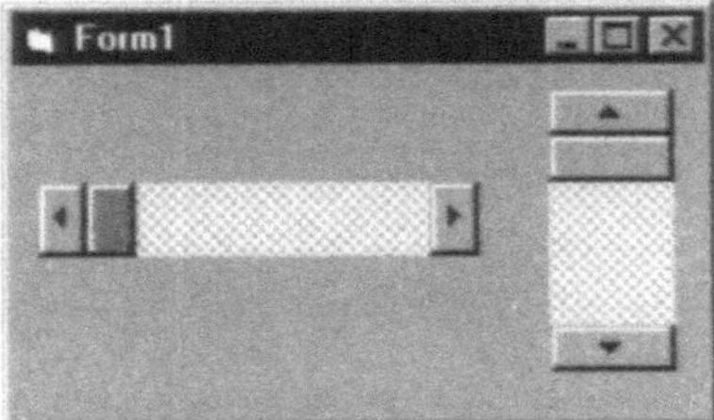

Fig. 5.9   Scroll bars.

- The first horizontal bar is called *Hscroll1*.
- The first vertical bar is called *Vscroll1*.
- The minimum value in a scroll bar is at the left/top.
- The maximum value in a scroll bar is at the right/bottom.

List Boxes

List boxes (fig. 5.10) allow the user to select items from a list. They act like small windows which show a few of the possible options available and allow the user to scroll the list.

List boxes and combo boxes are very similar in appearance but differ in their operation. In a list box the items are fixed by the program, for example, a list of files in a directory. The user can select an item by using the arrow keys to move to the appropriate item. The user can also search by typing in characters. The cursor is moved to the next item that has this character as the first character. If necessary, the search wraps from the end of the list to the beginning.

The first list box is called *List1*.

Fig. 5.10 *The* **ListBox** *control.*

Individual items in a list box can be referenced by using a subscript and the **List** property, for example, the third entry in a ListBox called *MyList* is *MyList.-*
List(3). The first entry is *MyList*.**List**(0).

The AddItem Method

Items can be added to a list in a list box or a combo box by using the **AddItem** method. The syntax of **AddItem** is:

*[form.] control.**AddItem** item[, index]*

- *item* is the item to be added to the list.
- *index* is the index where the item is to be added, The default is to add the item to the end of the list. The list index starts from zero.

For example:

*Country.**AddItem** "England"*
*Country.**AddItem** "Scotland"*
*Country.**AddItem** "Wales"*
*Country.**AddItem** "Northern Ireland"*

The program statements used to put items in a list are usually put into the procedure that loads the form containing the list.

The Sorted Property

The list box has a property called Sorted.

- If this is set to true then the order of the items in the list is alphabetically sorted at run-time; otherwise they appear in the order in which they were added to the list.

The use of the *index* field may interfere with the sort mechanism. The syntax of setting the **Sorted** property is:

*[form.]{ComboBox | ListBox}.**Sorted***

When the user clicks on a list box a selection can be made by scrolling through the list. The size of the list box is not expanded during the selection process.

Combo Boxes

There are three types of combo box:

- Simple combo.
- Drop-down combo.
- Drop-down list.

The type of combo box (fig. 5.11) is specified by changing the **Style** property for the box.

Fig. 5.11   ComboBox control.

All types of combo boxes are specified by the same button on the toolbox and named *Combo1, Combo2* and so on.

Individual elements in combo boxes can also be referenced by using the **List** property of the box, for example, the second entry in a combo box called *Combo1* is *Combo1.***List**(1).

The Simple Combo Box

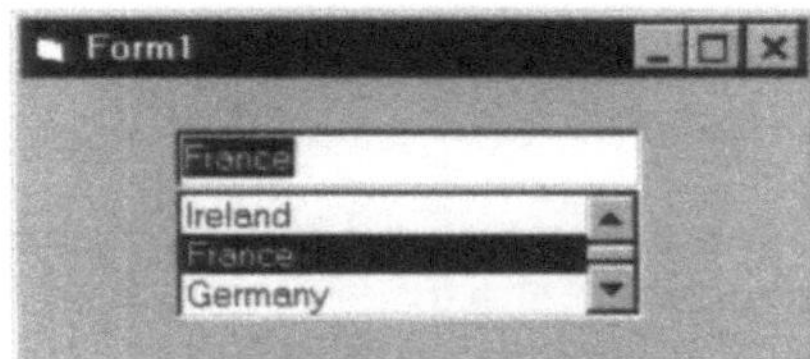

Fig. 5.12
Simple combo box.

The simple combo (fig. 5.12) looks like a text box, but has an "indented" list permanently displayed below it. The number of items is determined by the **Height** property.

The Drop-down Combo Box

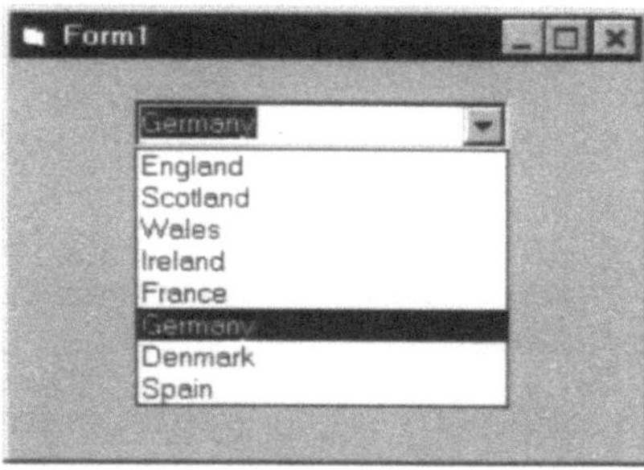

Fig. 5.13
Drop-down combo box.

   The drop-down combo (fig. 5.13) looks like a list box with an arrow separate from and to the right of the box. By clicking on the arrow, a range of options are shown below the box in a drop-down list.

   Both simple and drop-down combo boxes allow the user to select an option from the list. In addition, and in contrast to the list box and the drop-down list box, the user can type in text which the program may add to the list for future purposes.

The Drop-down Combo List

Fig. 5.14
Drop-down combo list.

   Drop-down lists (fig. 5.14) look like a text box with an arrow attached on the right. Clicking on the arrow causes a list of options to appear below the box in a similar way to the drop-down combo. The drop-down list behaves like a drop-down combo, except that the user must select from the list – the user cannot type in text.

The Timer Control

The timer (fig. 5.15) is given a time interval; when this interval has expired a timer event occurs.

Fig. 5.15   The **Timer** control.

- The maximum number of timers is 16.
- At design-time a timer is of fixed size.
- At run-time a timer is invisible.
- A user cannot access a **Timer** control.
- The **Interval** property is in milliseconds with a maximum value of 65,535.

Timers can be used, for example, periodically to save a file to disk in a word processor or to warn a user of a time deadline, or for simple animation or applications such as measuring reaction time.

Selecting Controls

- A single control can be selected by clicking on it.
- A group of controls can be selected by pressing the left mouse button on the form and dragging so that the group of controls that you want to select are enclosed in a box with a dotted outline.
- The enclosed controls can be moved as a single group.
- The controls can be deselected by clicking anywhere on the form.
- Controls that are scattered about the form can be selected to form a group by pressing and holding the **Ctrl** key while moving the mouse to each control and clicking the left button.

Setting Properties of Groups

Sometimes it is useful to set the properties of a group of controls together. This can be done by selecting the required properties. Only common properties are listed in the properties box. This facility is particularly useful for aligning and sizing controls.

The **Left** property of a group of controls can be set to the same value to ensure that they are all in the same vertical line.

The **Width** and **Height** properties ensure that they are all the same size.

Custom Controls

Custom controls are controls that are stored in a separate OCX file. There are two ways of making custom controls available. You must install them in your application, either by adding the name of the OCX file to your AUTOLOAD.VBP file, or by selecting the custom controls option from the **Tools** menu.

If you use the first option, the custom control will be available for every project you create – you will not have to install the custom files every time.

The CommonDialog Control

This is one of the most useful of the **CommonDialog** controls (fig. 5.16).

Fig. 5.16   The **CommonDialog** control.

The **CommonDialog** control displays six different dialog boxes (listed below), depending on which method is used. Four of these dialog boxes are shown in figs. 5.17 to 5.20.

Description	Method	Action value
No action	—	0
Displays **OpenDialogBox**	**ShowOpen**	1
Displays **SaveAsDialogBox**	**ShowSave**	2
Displays **ColorDialogBox**	**ShowColor**	3
Displays **FontDialogBox**	**ShowFont**	4
Displays **PrinterDialogBox**	**ShowPrinter**	5
Displays **HelpDialogBox**	**ShowHelp**	6

To display the open dialog box, use the command:

CommandDialog1.ShowOpen

For compatibility with earlier versions of Visual Basic when the **Action** property was used to achieve the same effect, you can also use the command:

CommonDialog1.Action = 1

The default name of the first common dialog box to be created is *Common-Dialog1*.

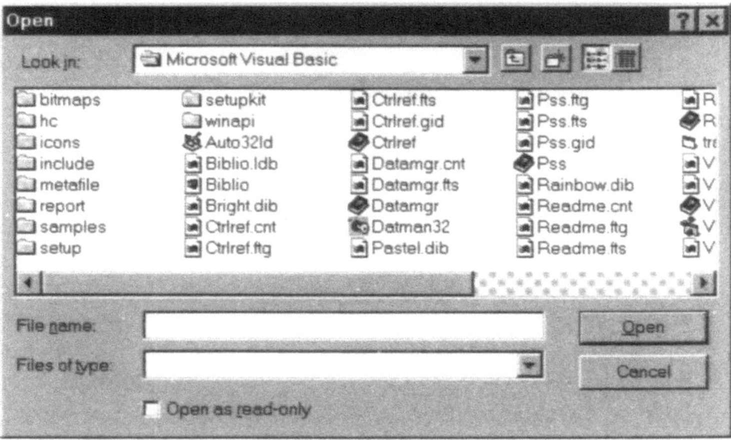

Fig. 5.17   The **OpenDialogBox**.

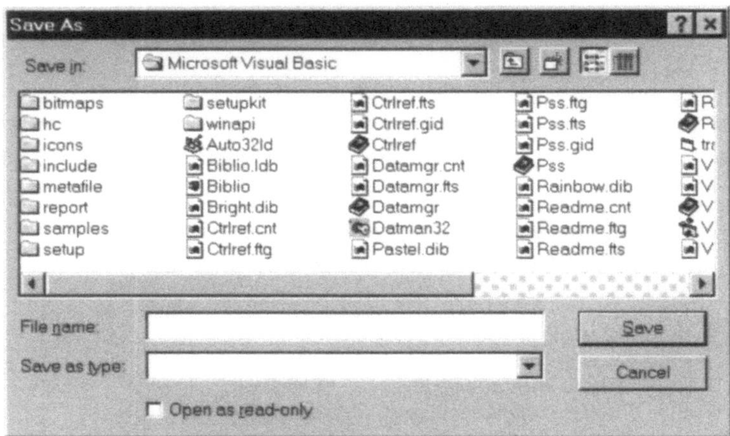

Fig. 5.18 The **SaveAsDialogBox**.

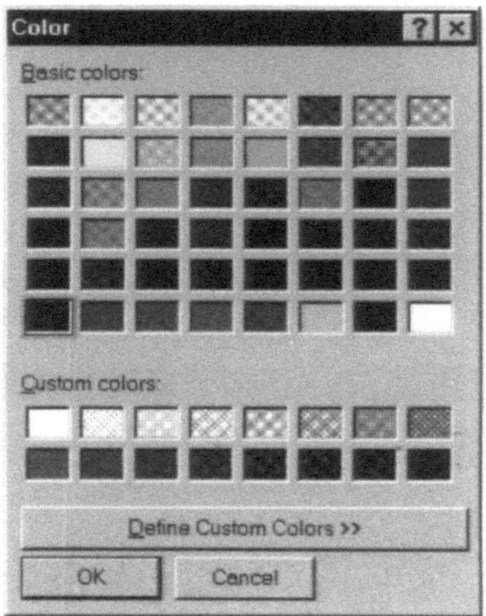

Fig. 5.19
The **ColorDialogBox**.

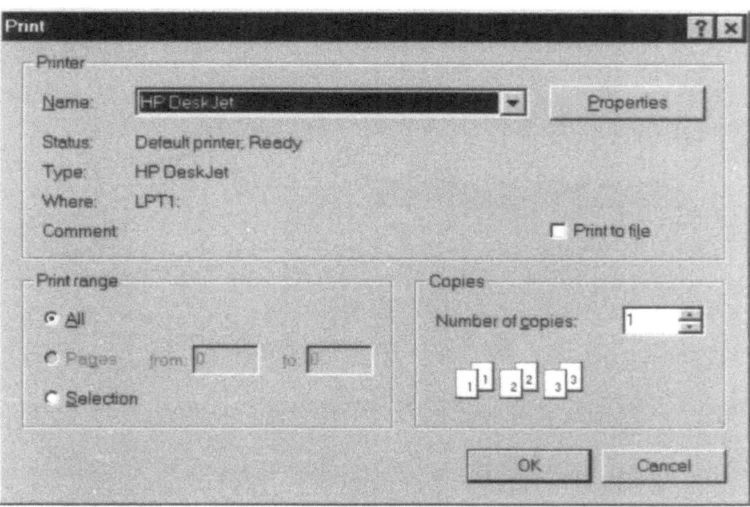

Fig. 5.20   The **PrinterDialogBox.**

Windows 95 automatically provides the **What's this** help button. Click the right mouse button over any control of the dialog and a **What's this** button appears. Click on it to obtain help information.

Click on the **Custom** property of the custom dialog control to see the properties specific to the method that can be applied. The dialog box shown in fig. 5.21 is displayed.

Fig. 5.21   The **CommonDialog** control properties.

The Slider Control

The **Slider** control (fig 5.22) behaves in the same way as a horizontal scroll bar and has very similar properties.

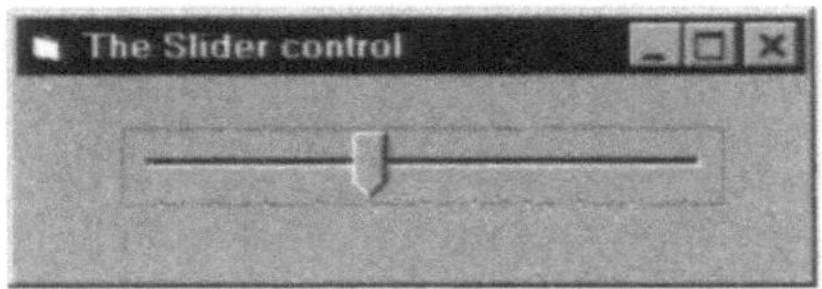

Fig. 5.22   The **Slider** control.

The properties **Min** and **Max** give the minimum and maximum values returned by the slider.

The **LargeChange** property gives the change in value of the slider when you click at either end of its run. The **SmallChange** property gives the change when you click between the end of the slider and the slider itself.

The StatusBar Control

The **StatusBar** control (fig. 5.23) consists of up to sixteen panels, each with its own set of properties. When this control is created it has only one panel. To add others or to insert text or a picture to a panel, click on the **PanelProperties** property.

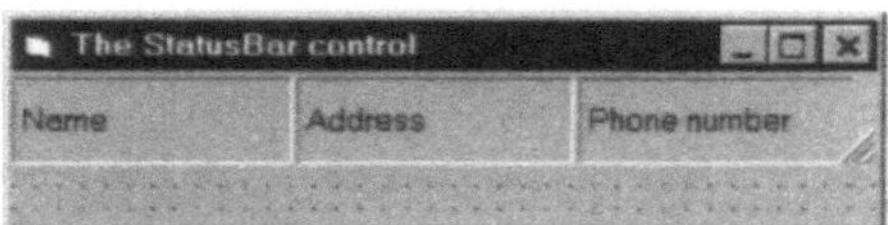

Fig. 5.23   The **StatusBar** control.

The **PanelProperty** dialog box is shown in fig. 5.24.

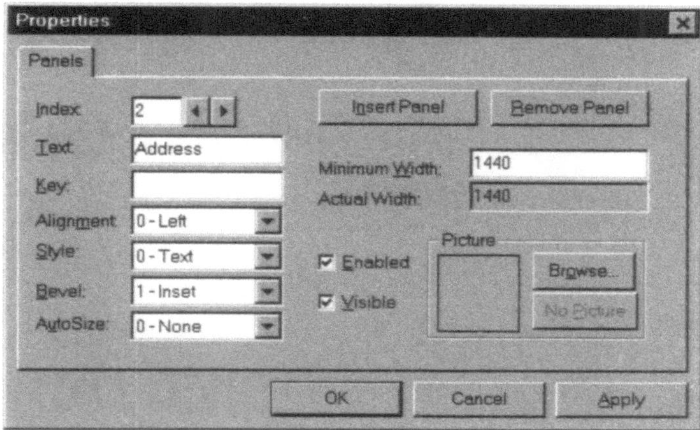

Fig. 5.24 *The* **PanelPropertiesdialog** *box.*

The panel can be aligned along any edge of the screen using the **Align** property.

6

The Insurance Quote Form

Introduction

This chapter shows how the controls introduced so far can be used. You will learn about:

- Designing a substantial form
- Using controls
- Developing event-driven software.

Design of the Quote Screen

The best way to gain familiarity with the Visual Basic controls is to design a substantial form that uses most of the major features that you have looked at. The form that you are going to look at is the sort of form that might be used by an insurance company when you ask for an insurance quote. The finished form is shown in fig. 6.1.

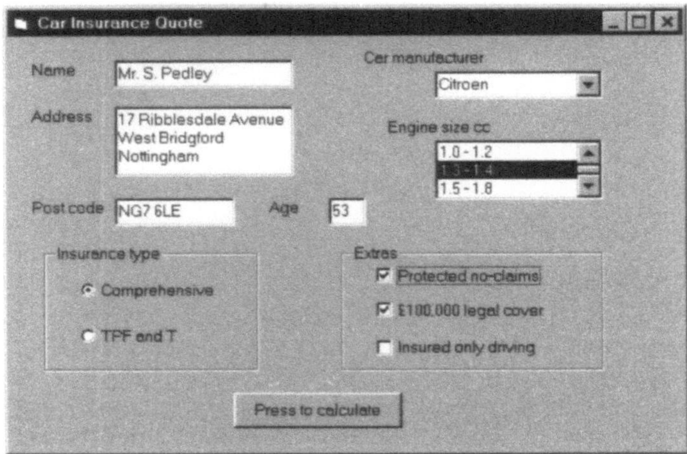

Fig. 6.1 *The car insurance quote form.*

- Start a new project.
- Change the title of the form, firstly by clicking on its **Properties** window to select it. Next, select the **Caption** property by clicking on it and alter it to *Car Insurance Quote.*
- Create the label *Name* by clicking on the label box in the toolbox. Move to the correct position, and press the left button on the mouse. As you drag the mouse, a rectangle appears. Release the button when it is about the right size.
- Make sure that the label box you have created is selected and click on its property box. Change the **Caption** property to "Name".
- Create the text box for the name.
- Change the **Text** property to "".
- Create the address and post code boxes in the same way.

Using Options Buttons

The insurance type has to be either comprehensive or third party and theft, so option buttons are used. Only one of a group of buttons can be selected.

- Create a frame.
- Insert the two option buttons.
- Change the **Caption** of the frame to *Insurance type.*
- Change the **Caption** of the top option button to *Comprehensive.*
- Change the **Caption** of the bottom option button to *TPF and T.*

Note: The frame must be created before the option buttons.

Creating Check Boxes

- Create a second frame for the check boxes.
- Change the caption of the frame to *Extras.*
- Add the three check buttons and change their captions to *Protected no-claims, £100,000 legal cover* and *Insured only driving.*

Creating Combo and List Boxes

The car manufacturer is selected by using a combo box. The user clicks on the left down arrow and a list of car manufacturers is displayed. A manufacturer is selected by clicking on it.

- Add the combo box.
- Change the **Text** property to "".
- Add a label box above the combo box and set its **Caption** property to *Car manufacturer.*
- Add the list box.

- Add a label box above the list box and set its **Caption** property to *Engine size.*
- Add the command button and change its **Caption** property to *Press to Calculate.*

Running the Program

The form is beginning to resemble the finished result. The program can be run by clicking on the run button in the toolbar.
Note the following points:

- Only one of the option buttons can be set at a time.
- Any number of check boxes can be set.
- Text can be typed into the text boxes; however, only one line of text can be put into the large address box.
- Text can be selected.
- The list and combo boxes are empty.

Initialising the List and Combo Box

The problem of the address box only accepting one line is solved by setting the **MultiLine** property of this text box to true.

- The combo and list boxes need to be initialised.

This can only be done at run-time. The best time is when the form is loaded.

- Double click on the form to go to the code associated with form loading and add the following text:

```
Private Sub Form_Load ( )
    list1.Additem "< 1.0"
    list1.AddItem " 1.0 - 1.2"
    list1.AddItem " 1.3 - 1.4"
    list1.AddItem " 1.5 - 1.8"
    list1.AddItem " 1.9 - 2.5"
    list1.AddItem "> 2.5"

    combo1.AddItem "Audi"
    combo1.AddItem "BMW"
    combo1.AddItem "Citroen"
    combo1.AddItem "Ford"
    combo1.AddItem "Peugeot"
    combo1.AddItem "Renault"
    combo1.AddItem "Rover"
```

```
        combo1.AddItem "Volvo"
        combo1.AddItem "Volkswagen"
End Sub
```

When the program is run, you can select an item from the list and combo boxes. However the combo box has *combo1*, its default text is displayed as shown in fig. 6.2.

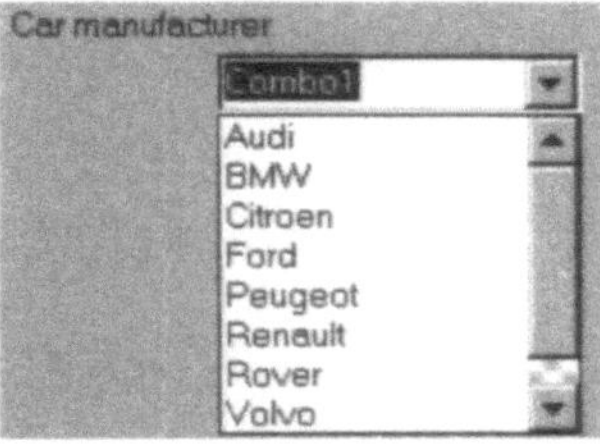

Fig. 6.2
Initialising the combo box.

To display one of the list items as a default, add the following line of code

```
combo1.ListIndex = 3
```

to the form load event handler. This will make *Ford* the default entry. *Audi* is the first item in the combo box and has a **ListIndex** property value of 0.

If you want a blank space displayed in place of a particular list item, assign **ListIndex** the value of − 1.

You can also assign the list box a default value, for example, by the statement:

```
list1.ListIndex = 2
```

When you have selected an item in a combo or list box, the value of the item you have selected is stored in the **Index** property. If no item is stored, this value is − 1.

TabIndex and TabStop

The user can move between controls by pressing the **Tab** button.

- The order is controlled by the **TabIndex** property of the controls.
- The control with the **TabIndex** value of 0 is read first, and so on.
- If you change one of the **TabIndex** values, all the other **TabIndex** values for the other controls are automatically adjusted.
- If you want a control to be skipped, you can set the value of its **TabStop** property to false.

7
Dialog Boxes

Introduction

Message and dialog boxes are used to give information to the user and to take in simple responses such as Yes or No. In this chapter you will learn how:

- To create and use message boxes.
- To create and use dialog boxes.

Creating a Message Box

Message and dialog boxes are windows that suspend processing of the previous window until the window in question is finished with.

- The user cannot access other windows of the current application until this window is complete.
- It is possible to access windows of other applications that are running.

The Message Box Function

A straightforward way of creating a dialog box is to use the pre-defined message box function (fig. 7.1). Options are available to set all the textual areas and to specify the buttons that are displayed:

Result = MsgBox (text, options, title)

- *Result* is the value returned by the function; this is optional.
- *text* is the message displayed.
- *options* is an integer that specifies the buttons and other attributes of the message box.

- *title* is the title displayed in the title bar.

For example:

*Response = **MsgBox** ("Ready to exit and save all data?")*

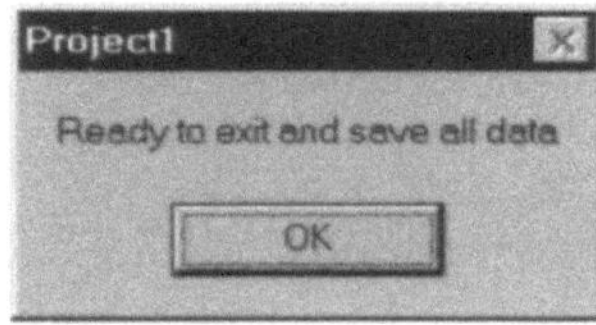

Fig. 7.1
The **MsgBox** function.

- The command button "OK" is automatically included.
- The message box is centred in the middle of the screen.

The Message Box Statement

The message box statement., MsgBox is similar to the message box function of the same name except that:

- The message box statement does not return any information about the button that is clicked.
- The brackets are omitted.

MsgBox text, options, title

- *Text* is the message displayed.
- *options* is an integer that specifies the buttons and other attributes of the message box.
- *title* is the title displayed in the title bar.

For example:

MsgBox "ready to exit and save all data"

Using Messages Boxes

To demonstrate how to use message boxes, the insurance quote form can be revisited.

If the user presses the command button to calculate the premiums and has not specified the age, post code, engine size, manufacturer or type of insurance cover, he should be informed that he has not yet provided all the required information.

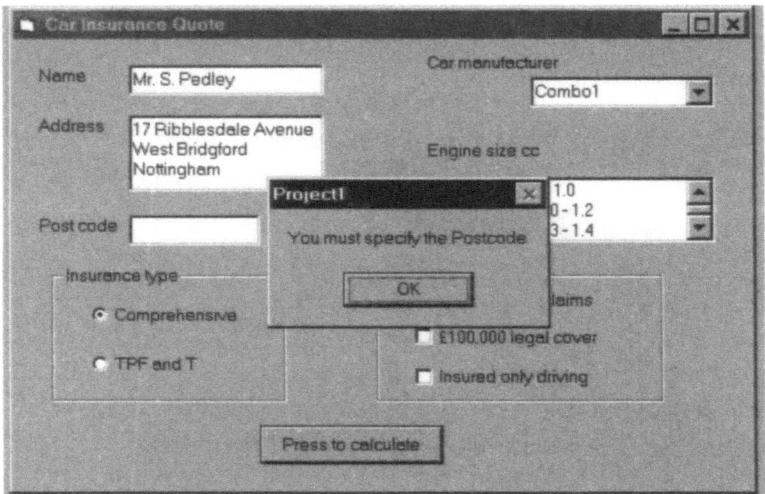

Fig. 7.2   *Using message boxes.*

A message box (fig. 7.2) to tell the user that he must specify the post code can be created as follows:

- Change the name of the post code text box from the meaningless *text3* to *PostCode*.
- Double click on the button; this takes you into the template subroutine which controls the button click event.
- Insert the following code to test if the post code has been input.

> *Private Sub Command1_Click ( )*
> *   If PostCode = "" Then MsgBox ("You must specify the Postcode")*
> *End Sub*

The same type of check can be used to make sure that the user has specified all the other required parameters.

- Change the names of the boxes to *Age, EngineSize* and *CarType.*
- Change the code that processes the button clicked event as shown:

> *Private Sub Command1_Click ( )*
> *   If PostCode = Then MsgBox ("You must specify the Postcode")*
> *   If Age = "" Then MsgBox ("You must specify your age")*
> *   If CarType = "" Then MsgBox ("You must specify the type of car")*
> *   If EngineSize = "" Then MsgBox ("You must specify the engine size")*

The user needs to specify whether one of the option buttons has been selected to indicate if *Comprehensive* or *Third party, fire and theft* is required.

- The option buttons take on the value true if set and false if not.

Change the name of the option buttons to *Comprehensive* and *TPFandT*. Put this code into the button click event processing:

*If Comprehensive = false **And** TPFandT = false **Then***
    ***MsgBox** ("You must specify the type of insurance cover")*
End If

Message Box Text

You can enter as much text as you want. The message box is the correct size and automatically puts in line feeds if necessary (fig. 7.3). If you are not satisfied with the format of text, you can control it by putting ASCII line feeds explicitly in your program.

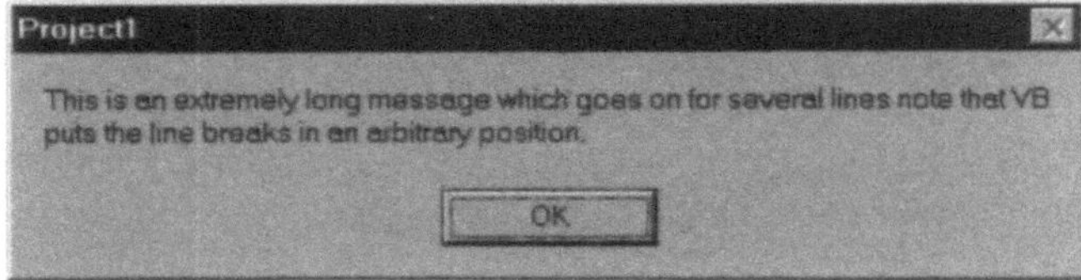

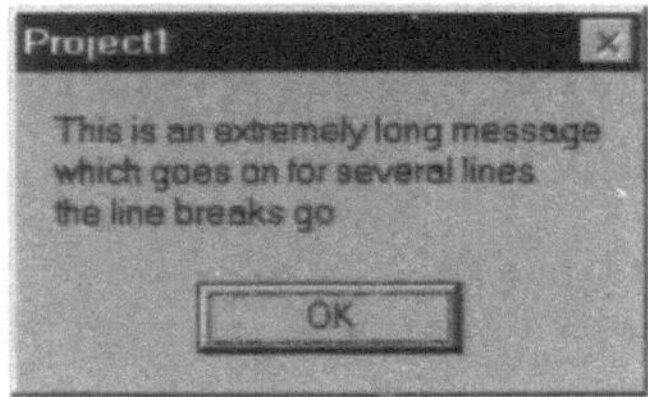

Fig. 7.3   *Message box text.*

*****Private Sub** Command1_Click ( )*
    M$ = "This is an extremely long message"
    *M$ = M$ + **Chr$**(10) + "which goes on for several lines"*
    *M$ = M$ + **Chr$**(10) + "I have explicitly chosen where"*
    *M$ = M$ + **Chr$**(10) + "the line breaks are"*
    ***MsgBox** M$*
End Sub

Chr$( ) is a Visual Basic function that prints the ASCII character corresponding to the number specified. For example, ASCII 10 indicates the linefeed character, and ASCII 13 is the carriage return character.

MsgBox Icons

There are four standard icons that you can include in your message boxes, by adding a type value after your message. These are useful for emphasising the significance of a message box.

A message box that informs the user that drivers under 21 are not insurable for cars with an engine size of over 2.5 litres (fig. 7.4) can be specified as

```
Private Sub EngineSize_Click ( )
    If Val(Age) < 21 And EngineSize = "> 2.5" Then
        MsgBox "Drivers under 21 are not insurable with this engine size", 16
    End If
    If Age = " " Then
        MsgBox "Must specify age first"
    End If
End Sub
```

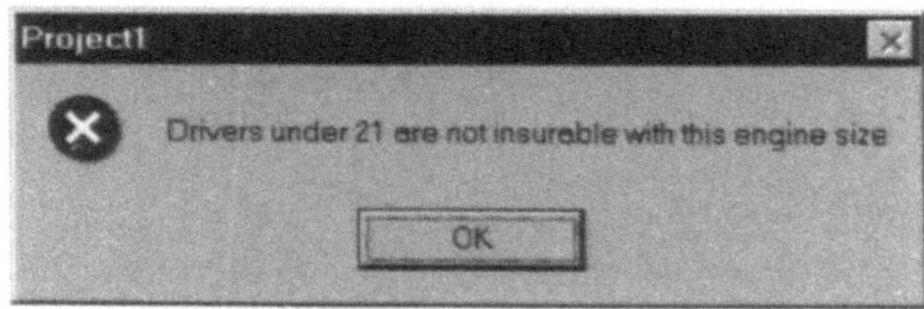

Fig. 7.4
Using the **MsgBox** icons.

Changing MsgBox Headers

The headers can be changed from the default project name by adding a third parameter after the type value:

```
Private Sub EngineSize_Click ( )
    If Val(Age) < 21 And EngineSize = "> 2.5" Then
        M$ = "Drivers under 21 "
        MS = M$ + Chr$(10) + "are not insurable with this engine size"
        MsgBox M$,16, "Uninsurable Driver Warning"
    End If
End Sub
```

As the addition of the header would make the line of code that displays the message box too long, the text to be displayed has been assigned to a text string M$ (fig. 7.5).

Fig. 7.5
Adding headers to message boxes.

The parameter of "16" in the **MsgBox** statement causes the Critical icon to be included in the message box. Symbolic names such as **vbCritical** are available in Visual Basic. Note if you are upgrading from Version 3 of Visual Basic that the names of these constants have been changed and there is no longer a need to include the file CONSTANT.TXT in your application, unless you wish to continue using the old constant names. The **Critical** icon replaces the old **Stop** icon.

Icon	Value	Name
Critical	16	**vbCritical**
Question mark	32	**vbQuestion**
Exclamation mark	48	**vbExplanation**
Information	64	**vbInformation**

MsgBox Buttons

Visual Basic also allows you to specify what buttons you want to have in your message box (fig. 7.6). As a default it puts in the OK button. The buttons are specified by adding a number to the type parameter.

Buttons	Value	Name
OK	0	**vbOKOnly**
OK, Cancel	1	**vbOKCancel**
Abort, Retry, Ignore	2	**vbAbortRetryIgnore**
Yes, No, Cancel	3	**vbYesNoCancel**
Yes, No	4	**vbYesNo**
Retry, Cancel	5	**vbRetryCancel**

The code shown below will display a question mark icon and the **Abort, Retry** and **Ignore** buttons:

```
Private Sub Command1_Click ( )
MsgBox "Error on reading disk", 32 + 2, "Disk error"
End Sub
```

It would be better to use the code:

```
Private Sub Command1_Click ( )
    MsgBox "Error on reading disk", vbQuestion + vbAbortRetryIgnore, "Disk
    error"
End Sub
```

Fig. 7.6
Adding buttons to message boxes.

Getting Button Input

Visual Basic provides a mechanism to let your program know what button the user has selected:

> *Private Sub Command1_Click ( )*
>   *Response = MsgBox ("Continue", vbQuestion + vbAbortRetryIgnore)*
> *End Sub*

The value of *Response* indicates the button pressed.

To get button input, the **MsgBox** function rather than the **MsgBox** statement is used. In common with all functions, a value is returned. In this case the value returned indicates what button the user has selected.

Note: The parameters to the **MsgBox** function are enclosed in parentheses, whereas the **MsgBox** statement parameters are not.

Button Pressed	Value	Name
OK	1	**vbOK**
Cancel	2	**vbCancel**
Abort	3	**vbAbort**
Retry	4	**vbRetry**
Ignore	5	**vbIgnore**
Yes	6	**vbYes**
No	7	**vbNo**

The Input Box Function

If the user has to input something other than pressing one of the buttons, the function **InputBox$** is used (fig. 7.7).

> *InputBox$ (Prompt, Title, Default, Left, Top)*

- *Prompt* is the string that is displayed in the dialog box.
- *Title* is the title in the dialog box's title bar.
- *Default* is the initial text placed in the text box.
- *Left* is the distance from the left edge of the screen to the dialog box.
- *Top* is the distance from the top of the screen to the top of the dialog box.

InputBox$ always has the buttons OK and Cancel.

> *Private Sub Command1_Click ( )*
>   *FileName = InputBox("What is the file name")*
> *End Sub*

Fig. 7.7
Using InputBox.

Specifying Default Text

Headers and text can both be specified to message boxes using the **InputBox** function (fig. 7.8) by adding two additional parameters:

> *Private Sub Command1_Click ( )*
>   *Header$ = "File Input"*
>   *FileName = InputBox("File name?", Header$, "project.txt")*
> *End Sub*

Fig. 7.8
Specifying a header and using a default input.

InputBox$ always returns a string, however the **InputBox** function returns a value of type **Variant**.

8
Operators and Variables

Introduction

Visual Basic offers a wide range of different data types and powerful operators for manipulating them. In this chapter you will learn about:

- Data types.
- The range of data types.
- Declaring variables.
- Static variables.
- Global variables.
- Arithmetic operators.
- Integer division.
- The **Mod** operator.
- The comparison operators.
- String operators.
- Logical operators.

Data Types

This version of the Basic language seems surprisingly powerful for those who only have memory of the Basics available on early microcomputers. It offers a wide range of data types and operators.

In Basic it is not necessary to declare a variable before it is used. This has the advantage of allowing you to make up variables as you go along and as they are needed. The main disadvantage to this is that a spelling mistake may create a new variable instead of indicating a typing error.

The **Type** of a variable can be indicated by a suffix which follows the name; for example, **sum%** is an integer, while **sum$** is a string.

Type	Size in bytes	Suffix
Integer	2	%
Long	4	&
Single	4	!
Double	8	#
Currency	8	@
String	dependent on string size	$
Variant	dependent on type of data stored	None

The **Variant** data type takes on the form of the data that it is asked to store. For example, if a string is assigned to a **Variant** type, the **Variant** type takes on the **String** data type. If it is assigned a numeric value, it takes on that type and can be used in calculations.

Variants should be used with great care.

Range of Data Types

The **Single** and **Long** types are real, floating point types which approximate to the number being represented. In an accounting system, the **Currency** type should be used, to avoid rounding errors.

Type	Most Negative	Most Positive
Integer	−32,768	32,767
Long	−2,147,483,648	2,147,483,647
Single	−3.402 823 E38	3.402 823 E38
Double	−1.797 693 134 862 32 E308	1.797 693 134 862 32 E308
Currency	−922,337,203,685,477·5808	922,337,203,685,477·5807
String	0 characters	approx. 65,000 characters

Declaring Variables

Virtually all modern languages require variables to be declared prior to their first reference, where the user explicitly states the name and type of any variable to be used. In Basic the **Dim** statement is used to declare variables.

For example:

> *Dim Count As Integer, Money As Currency*

Note:	*Dim Count, NewCount As Integer* is incorrect since it declares *NewCount* as an integer but not *Count.*

> *Dim identifier As type, identifier As type*

If it a good idea to make variable declaration mandatory by either:

- Selecting the **Environment** page from the **Options** option on the **Tools** menu and selecting the **Require Variable Declaration** option.
- If you only want to force explicit declarations in one module, put the following line into the declarations section of the module

Option Explicit

Static Variables

There are a number of other issues to be considered when you are declaring a variable. A variable declared within a procedure is initialised every time the procedure is entered. However, if you want a variable to retain its value and not be re-initialised, the **Static** keyword must be used:

Static identifier As type

Note: The **Dim** keyword is replaced by **Static**.

For example:

Static MyName As String

Variables Scope

Variables can be declared in modules, forms or procedures.

- A variable declared in a procedure is only available for use within that procedure – even if it has been declared **Static**.
- A variable declared within the general section of a form has scope throughout that form.

The scope of variables declared at module level depends on the keyword used to declare it:

- If a variable is declared with **Dim** it has scope throughout the module.
- If a variable is declared as **Global** it is available throughout the program:

Global identifier As type

Note: The **Dim** keyword is replaced.

For example:

Global YourName As String

Arithmetic Operations

Much of the use of operators is similar to other programming languages, however it is worthwhile reviewing them here as there may be a few surprises.

There are seven arithmetic operations:

Operator	Action	Example
+	Addition	2 + 3 = 5
−	Subtraction	9 − 2 = 7
*	Multiplication	1.5 * 3 = 4.5
/	Division	11 / 2 = 5.5
^	Exponentiation	2 ^ 3 = 8
\	Integer Division	6 \ 1.6 = 3
Mod	Modulus	7 Mod 2 = 1

Integer Division

Integer division (\) gives the integer result of dividing the numbers concerned after all of them have been rounded.

For example:

$$7 \setminus 1.2 \rightarrow 7 \setminus 1 \rightarrow 7$$
$$7 \setminus 1.6 \rightarrow 7 \setminus 2 \rightarrow 3$$

The Mod Operator

The **Mod** operator gives the remainder after interger division, for example:

$$8.5 \; Mod \; 3 \rightarrow 9 \; Mod \; 3 \rightarrow 0$$
$$8.4 \; Mod \; 2.5 \rightarrow 8 \; Mod \; 3 \rightarrow 2$$

The Comparison Operator

The standard set of comparison operators are provided.

Operator	Action
=	Equal
<	Less than
>	Greater than
<=	Less than or equal
>=	equal
<>	Not equal

String Concatenation

One of the strong features of Visual Basic is the ease with which strings can be manipulated. Strings can be compared and also added together (concatenated). For example:

```
FirstName$ = "John"
LastName$ = "Smith"
MyName$ = FirstName$ + " " & LastName$
```

The variable *MyName$* contains "John Smith".

Both the "+" and "&" operators can be used to concatenate strings. If the operands are of mixed type a different result may occur; for example, addition of the operands instead of concatenation.

For example:

```
x = "7"
y = "8"
Print x+y, x&y
x = 7
Print x+y, x&y
```

produces the following results:

```
78          78
15          78
```

The Logical Operators

The logical operators, such as **And**, allow you to use Boolean logic and give a final output of true (-1) or false (0).

Operator	Action
And	And
Eqv	Equivalent
Imp	Implication
Or	Or
Xor	Exclusive or
Not	Not

The And Operator

The **And** operator returns a value of true only if both operands are true.

A	B	A And B
true	true	true
true	false	false
false	true	false
false	false	false

For example:

> *If (Age < 35) **And** (Salary > 40000) **Then***
> > ***MsgBox** "You are a Yuppie"*
> *End If*

If you are under 35 and earn over £40,000, you are a yuppie.

The Eqv Operator

The **Eqv** (logical equivalence) operator returns a true value when the operands are the same, otherwise it returns false.

A	B	A Eqv B
true	true	true
true	false	false
false	true	false
false	false	true

For example:

> *If Age **Eqv** 18 **Then***
> > ***MsgBox** "You can vote"*
> *End If*

Where numeric values are used, **Eqv** has the same effect as the equals sign. **Eqv** does not perform as a comparison operator for strings.

The Imp Operator

The **Imp** (implication) operator returns a true value unless the first value is true and the second is false; that is, it is true if either the first operand is false or the second operand is true.

A	B	A Imp B
true	true	true
true	false	false
false	true	true
false	false	true

For example:

> *If (Age < 21) **Imp** (CarEngineSize < 2000) **Then***
> > ***MsgBox** "Low Risk Driver"*
> ***Else***
> > ***MsgBox** "High Risk Driver"*
> ***End If***

Drivers who are under 21 and drive a car with an engine size of 2 litres or over are high risk drivers.

The Or Operator

The **Or** operator returns the result true if either of the operands are true, including the case where both of the operands are true.

A	B	A Or B
true	true	true
true	false	true
false	true	true
false	false	false

For example:

> *If (Hobby = "Alligator wrestling") **Or** (Hobby = "Insulting bouncers") **Then***
> > ***MsgBox** "You are living dangerously"*
> ***End If***

If you like insulting bouncers or wrestling alligators, you are living dangerously.

The Xor Operator

The **Xor** (exclusive **Or**) operator is true if either operand is true; it is false if both operands are the same, either both false or both true.

The **Xor** operator is similar to the **Or** operator except that, if both A and B are true, the result is false.

A	B	A Xor B
true	true	false
true	false	true
false	true	true
false	false	false

For example:

> *If (TrafficLight = "red") **Xor** (TrafficLight = "green") **Then***
> >   ***MsgBox** "The traffic lights are working"*
> *Else*
> >   ***MsgBox** "The traffic lights are not working"*
> *End If*

The Not Operator

The **Not** operator is a unitary operator, that is, it needs only one operand. If the operand is true it produces false. If the operand is false it produces true.

A	Not A
true	false
false	true

For example:

> *If **Not** (animal = "carnivore") **Then***
> >   ***MsgBox** "The animal is a herbivore or omnivore"*
> *End If*

9
Controlling Program Flow

Introduction

Program flow statements allow the program to perform different things based upon the testing of values. It is this feature that allows computers apparently to make choices. In this chapter you will learn about:

- **If...Then...Else** statements.
- **Select Case** statements.
- **Switch** statement.
- **GoTo** statement.

Types of Program Control

There are three constructs that can be used to control program flow:

- **If...Then** statement.
- **Select Case** structure.
- **GoTo** statement.

These are similar to most modern languages; however, there are a few important differences.

The If...Then...Else Statement

This statement exists in two forms: single line and multi-line. The simplest form of the **If...Then** statement is the single line:

*If condition **Then** statement*

For example:

> *If (Age < 18)* **Then MsgBox** *"You cannot vote yet"*

If *Age* is less than 18, a message box is displayed stating that *"you cannot vote yet"*. If the *Age* is 18 or more, then no action is taken. An **Else** clause can be added:

> *If condition* **Then** *statement* **Else** *statement*

For example:

> *If (Age < 18)* **Then MsgBox** *"You cannot vote yet"* **Else MsgBox** *"You can vote"*

In this statement if the *Age* is 18 or more, the message *"You can vote"* is shown. The multi-line version of the statement is a little more complicated:

> *If condition* **Then**
>   *statements*
> **Else If** *condition* **Then**
>   *statements*
> **Else**
>   *statements*
> *End If*

For example:

> *If (BankBalance < 0)* **Then**
>   **MsgBox** *"Overdrawn"*
> *Else*
>   **MsgBox** *"In credit"*
> *End If*

If the condition (*BankBalance < 0*) is true, then *Overdrawn* is displayed; if it is not, then *In credit* is displayed.

Note: The word **Then** must be on the same line as **If**.
       The need for **End If** if the **If** statement is longer than one line.

Nested Ifs

If statements can be nested to make multiple levels of decision, for example:

> *If (Age < 21)* **Then**
>   *If (EngineSize >= 2000)* **Then**
>   *If (DrivingStyle = "Reckless")* **Then**

```
        MsgBox "An accident is likely"
      End If
   End If
End If
```

If possible, avoid using nested **Ifs** of this type; they are very confusing. Better code for the above example would be:

```
If (Age < 21) And (EngineSize >= 2000) And (DrivingStyle="Reckless") Then
     MsgBox "An accident is likely"
End If
```

Note: The **And** and **Or** clauses need to be on the same line as the **If** and **Then** words.

The Else If Clause

Multiple **Else** clauses can also be used. For example:

```
If animal = "rabbit" Then
     food = "lettuce"
Else If animal = "lion" Then
     food = "meat"
Else If animal = "cat" Then
     food = "Smoked salmon"
End If
```

The Select Case Structure

The **Select Case** construction is useful when there are several consequences dependent on the result of one expression.

The syntax of **Select Case** is:

```
Select Case testexpression
    Case expressionlist1
         statementblock1
    Case expressionlist2
         statementblock2

    ...
    [Case Else
         statementblockn]
End Select
```

The previous example can be coded as shown below:

```
Select Case animal
     Case "rabbit"
          food = "lettuce"
     Case "lion"
          food = "meat"
     Case "cat"
          food = "Smoked salmon"
End Select
```

At each **Case** statement, four different types of expression can be used:

- A string or numeric expression.
- An explicit value.
- A range using the keyword **To.**
- A conditional range using the keyword **Is.**

For example:

```
Select Case Speed
     Case 0, 1, 2
          MsgBox "Driving a little slow"
     Case 3 To 30
          MsgBox "Driving within legal limits"
     Case 31 To 40
          MsgBox "Driving a little too fast"
     Case Is > 40
          MsgBox "Driving much too fast"
End Select
```

- **Case 0,1,2** means if the *Speed* is 0, 1, or 2 display the message *Driving a little slow.*
- **Case 3 To 30** applies if *Speed* is in the range 3–30.
- **Case Is > 40** applies if *Speed* is greater than 40.

The Switch Function

The **Switch** function is useful if you want to set one variable according to the result of a hierarchy of tests:

```
variable = Switch (cond1, expr1... [, cond7, expr7])
```

For example:

```
Food = Switch (animal = "rabbit", "lettuce", animal = "lion", "meat")
```

If the animal is a rabbit, the variable string *Food* is assigned the value *lettuce*. If it is a lion, the food is *meat*. Visual Basic tests the conditions from left to right. When it meets a true condition, it does not proceed any further.

Note: There can be a maximum of seven conditions in a **Switch** function. If none of the conditions are true, there is no assignment.

The GoTo Statement

GoTo unconditionally transfers control to a specified label. The **GoTo** statement has proved to be the most unpopular statement in modern programming languages, as you can usually remove the need for a **GoTo** statement using other programming statements. It is usually good practice to avoid using this statement, however it can be useful if a error occurs, in order to jump straight to the error handler.

GoTo label

Labels are identifiers with a colon suffix.
For example:

    ...
If ErrorNumber <> 0 Then GoTo ErrorHandler
    ...

    ...
ErrorHandler:

Note: The *ErrorHandler* label is indicated by an appended colon.

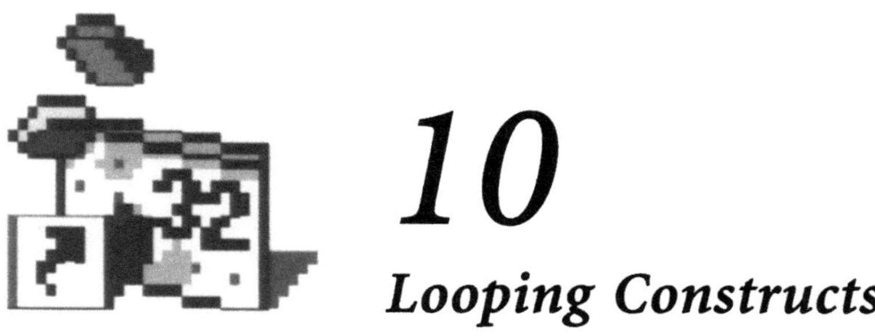

10
Looping Constructs

Introduction

Looping constructs are used when the same set of steps has to be carried out many times. There is usually a counter that indicates how many times the loop is executed, or a test that is made every time the loop is executed to see if it should be executed again. In this chapter you will learn about these looping constructs:

- **Do...Loop** construct.
- **Exit Do** statement.
- **While...Wend** construct.
- **For... Step... Next** construct.
- **Exit For** statement.

Types of Looping Constructions

There are three looping constructs in Visual Basic:

- **Do...Loop**
- **While...Wend**
- **For...Next.**

The Do...While Clause

The **Do...Loop** construct allows you to execute a block of code if the specified condition is met.

> *Do While condition*
>   *statements*
> *Loop*

For example:

```
Count = 0
Do While count < Number_of_members
    Print_letter( );
    Count = Count + 1
Loop
```

This example could be used to print a letter to send to the members of a group. A *Count* is initialised to zero. A check is made at the start of the loop to see if *Count* is less than the number of members; if it is the letter is printed and the *Count* is incremented. The loop is repeated until a letter has been printed for every member.

Another form of the **Do...While** statement is to have the **While** condition at the end of the loop:

```
Do
    Statements
Loop While condition
```

For example:

```
Count = 0
Do
    Print_letter( );
    Count = Count + 1
Loop While count < Number_of_members
```

This example will do the same as the previous example. The difference is that in this form the loop will always be executed once – since the test is made at the end of the loop. If the *Numbers_of_members* was zero, the first example would not print any letters, while the second example would.

The Do...Until Clause

This looping construct is very similar in function to the **Loop...While** construct.

```
Do Until condition
    statements
Loop
```

For example:

```
Count = 0
Do Until count >= Number_of_members
    Print_letter( );
    Count = Count + 1
Loop
```

This example prints a letter until the *Count* is greater or equal to the *Number_of_members*. A variant of this construct is to put the condition at the end of the loop.

```
Do
    statements
Loop Until condition
```

For example:

```
Count = 0
Do
    Print_letter( );
    Count = Count + 1
Loop Until count >= Number_of_members
```

This is functionally the same as the first example, except that the loop is always executed one.

Exit Do Statement

Loops can be aborted using the **Exit Do** construct. but it is not good programming practice and can make programs difficult to understand and to debug.

```
Count = 0
Do While Count < Number_of_members
    Error = Print_letter()
    If Error = true Then
        Exit Do
    End If
    Count = Count + 1
Loop
```

The *Print_letter* routine returns an error code, perhaps indicating that the printer is out of paper or not working. If this is the case, the program exits from the loop that is printing the letters.

Note: The **Exit Do** leaves the loop and jumps to the line after the **Loop** statement.

If there are nested loops, the **Exit Do** construct jumps to the next loop level, not out of all the nested loops.

For example:

```
Xcount = 0
Ycount = 0
```

```
Do While Xcount < 512
    Do While Ycount < 512
        If Picture (Xcount, Ycount) < Threshold Then Exit Do
        End If
    Ycount = Ycount + 1
    Loop
Xcount = Xcount + 1
Loop      'Jump to this statement from the if statement if the condition is met
```

This program example checks each pixel of a 512 × 512 picture which is stored in an array. If the **Exit Do** is executed, the program only jumps out of the current loop being executed.

Note: A comment is preceded by a single quote mark or by the keyword **Rem**, which is short for remark.

The While...Wend Clause

The **While...Wend** clause is functionally the same as the **Do While...Loop** form of **Do...Loop**, and is similar in syntax to **While** loops in other languages.

```
Count = 0
While count < Number_of_members
    Print_letter( );
    Count = Count + 1
Wend
```

The **Exit Do** facility is not available in **While...Wend** and has no equivalent.

The For...Next Construct

The **For...Next** construct has an integral loop counter. The syntax is:

```
For counter = start To end [Step increment]
    [statementblock]
    [Exit For]
    [statementblock]
Next [counter [, counter]]
```

For example:

```
For Count = 1 To Number_of_members
    Print_letter( )
Next Count
```

This prints a letter to each member and automatically increments the loop counter *Count*. The amount by which the counter is changed every time it loops is indicated by the **Step** construct. The default step value is 1.

> *For Count = 0 To 10 Step 2*
>   *MsgBox Count*
> *Next Count*

This prints out 0, 2, 4, 6, 8, 10. The loop value is then changed until it exceeds the terminating value.

The **Step** value can also be negative, in which case the counter is decremented.

> *For Count = 10 To 2 Step –3*
>   *MsgBox Count*
> *Next Count*

This prints out the values 10, 7, 4.

At the start of the next loop, the value of *Count* is 1; as it is less that the terminating value, the loop therefore terminates.

Note: The variable *Count* can be omitted after the keyword **Next** – but it is advisable to put it in, particularly if using nested **For...Next** loops.

Terminating For Loops

Next can be used to terminate several loops at the same time by listing several variable counters:

> *For X = 1 To 10*
>   *For Y = 1 To 20*
>   *Value[X, Y] = true*
> *Next Y, X*

As can be seen in the example, the use of **Next** to terminate several loops at the same time is not very aesthetic from the point of view of the textual layout. When reviewing the document, there appears to be fewer lines than expected and an indentation level appears not to be correctly terminated. For these reasons, anyone using this construct should be very careful and consider other people who may be reviewing the program at a later date.

Exit For

The **Exit For** construct can only be used from within a **For** loop and is a way of leaving the loop immediately:

```
For Count = 1 To Number_of_members
    Error = Print_letter()
    If Error = true Then
        Exit For
    End If
Next Count
```

One of the major run-time problems when developing an application is that endless loops can occur if the end conditions are never met. It is not advisable to modify the loop counter within the loop for this reason.

11
Using Data Structures

Introduction

In this chapter you will learn:

- How to create and use arrays.
- How to define new data structures.

Arrays

The most common form of data structure is the array, which is a way of collecting together similar items of the same data type. For example, a list of employee salaries can be saved as a one-dimensional array of type **Currency**, while, for example, a holiday chart can be saved as a two-dimensional array. Unlike most languages, Visual Basic also allows you to amend the dimensions of arrays at run-time.

Declaring Arrays

Before an array can be used, it must be declared using the **Dim** statement:

> **Dim** *name (subscripts) [As type] [, ...]*

One-Dimensional Arrays

The simplest arrays have only one dimension, for example:

> **Dim** *MyList(5)*

This defines a one-dimensional array with six elements, *MyList(0)* to *MyList(5)*. The statement

    Dim *MyList(0* **To** *5)*

is equivalent.

Multi-Dimensional Arrays

In arrays with more than one dimension, both lower and upper bounds must be specified. The following are all equivalent:

    Dim *A (8, 3)*
    Dim *A (0* **To** *8, 0* **To** *3)*
    Dim *A (8, 0* **To** *3)*

The array defined looks like this:

0,0	0,1	0,2	0,3	0,4	0,5	0,6	0,7	0.8
1,0	1,1	1,2	1,3	1,4	1,5	1,6	1,7	1,8
2,0	2,1	2,2	2,3	2,4	2,5	2,6	2,7	2,8
3,0	3,1	3,2	3,3	3,4	3,5	3,6	3,7	3,8

If not specified, the lower bound of an array is 0. The maximum number of dimensions in an array is 60.

    Dim *Salary (55)* **As Currency**

- This defines an array called *Salary.*
- The first element of the array is *Salary (0).*
- The final element of the array is *Salary (55).*
- The type of each element of the array is **Currency.**

If you do not want the first element of the array to be 0, you can specify the lower limit.

    Dim *Year (1980* **To** *1995)*

- The first element of this array is *Year (1980).*
- The final element is *Year (1995).*

Re-dimensioning Arrays

Visual Basic is unusual in that the range of previously defined arrays can be changed, using the **ReDim** statement, while the program is executing.

Dim Year (1980 To 1996) As Integer

...

...

ReDim Year (1978 To 1996)

...

First = 1920
Last = 1940
ReDim Year (First To Last)

The **ReDim** statement changes the number of elements so that the first is 1978 and the last is 1996. Later it changes the limits to 1920 and 1940.

Note: The type of the array cannot be changed.

If you want to preserve values already in the array, you need to use the optional keyword **Preserve**, otherwise they will be erased.

Dim Year (1980 To 1996) As Integer

...

...

ReDim Preserve Year (1980 To 2000)

Note: If you use **Preserve**, you can only change the dimension of the final element.

Multi-Dimensional Arrays

A table such as the one shown below showing the unit cost of disk drives depending on the number bought and the quantity purchased can be represented in a two-dimensional array.

Quantity Ordered →					
		1	2	2-5	5-10
Model ↓	STC104	200	180	170	150
	STC202	300	270	250	240
	STC307	400	360	340	320

Dim Cost (0 To 3, 0 To 2)

or

Dim Cost (3, 2)

The two **Dim** statements are the same. The cost of two STC307 disk drives is given by element Cost(1,2).

User-Defined Data Types

Sometimes it is useful to group together information, for example, if you are maintaining employee records in a company:

Name	Age	Salary
Jim	34	17,000
Sally	28	29,000
Duncan	57	23,000

Each row of the table can be grouped together by means of a user-defined data type defined by the **Type** statement:

```
Type Person
      Name As String
      Age As Integer
      Salary As Currency
End Type


Dim Staff (2) As Person
```

- You can refer to Sally's salary by *Staff (1).Salary.*
- Arrays declared within a user-defined type must have their dimensions explicitly declared, that is, not in a variable. A user-defined type cannot contain a dynamic array.

If user-defined types are used within an array, they cannot be redefined at run-time using **ReDim**.

The Erase Statement

If you want to free the memory space taken up by a dynamic array, you can use the **Erase** statement:

```
Erase arrayname [, arrayname]
Dim Year (1978 To 1994) As Integer
Dim Age (92) As Integer

...

...
Erase Year, Age
```

- The **Erase** statement frees the space allocated to the arrays called *Year* and *Age*.

- For static arrays, the space is not recovered. Instead, **Erase** sets the elements of the array to "empty" values.
- Numeric array: **Erase** sets each element to zero.
- String static array: **Erase** sets each element to an empty string ("").
- Array of user-defined types: **Erase** sets all elements to 0, including fixed string elements.

12
Menus

Introduction

Menus are a key feature of virtually all Windows programs. Fortunately, Visual Basic provides a set of tools that allow you to define the menus that you want in an interactive way. In this chapter you will learn:

- How to create and amend menus
- How to use short-cut keys to invoke menu items
- How to disable and enable menu items.

Using Menu Bars

Menu bars (fig. 12.1) are a common feature of Windows applications.

The menu bar

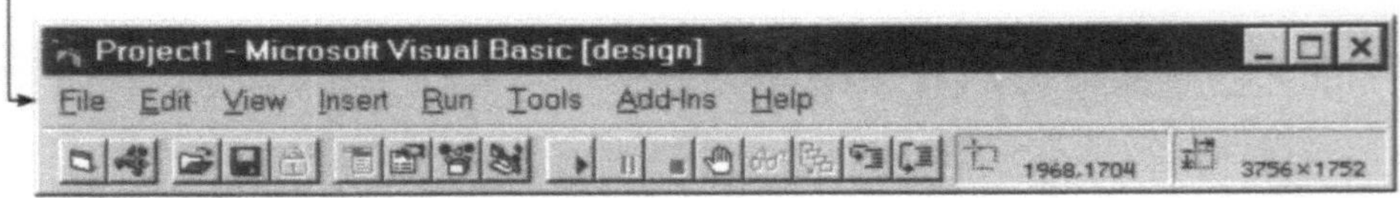

Fig. 12.1   *The menu bar.*

Menus appear on the menu bar at the top of the window. Clicking on a menu name causes the elements of the menu to drop down.

Menus can be easily created in Visual Basic. The car insurance quote program can be improved by adding a menu bar with two items, *File* and *Help*. When these menus are pulled down they give the options shown in fig. 12.2.

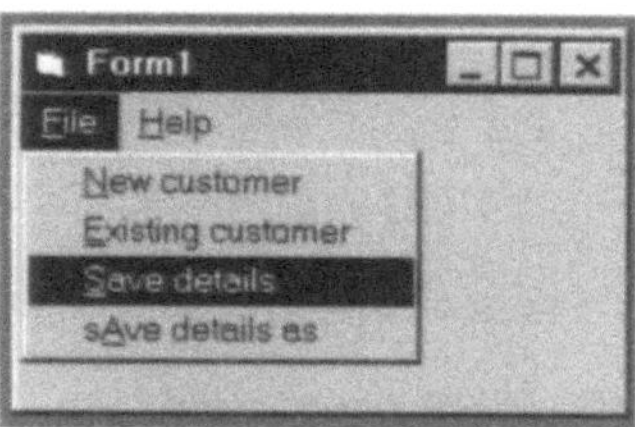
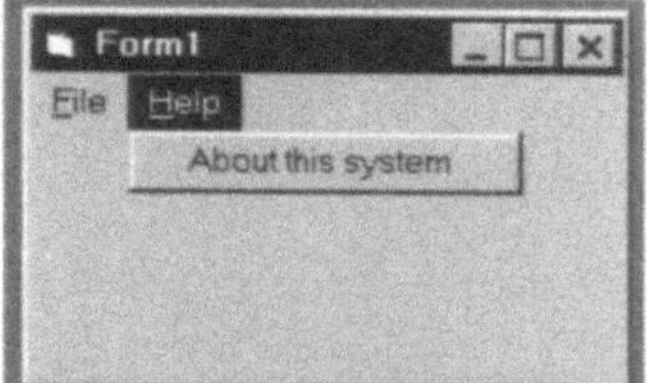

Fig. 12.2 *The completed menu.*

To create a menu, click on the menu editor icon on the toolbar as shown in fig. 12.3.

Fig. 12.3 *The menu editor icon.*

The menu editor dialog box is displayed as shown in fig. 12.4.

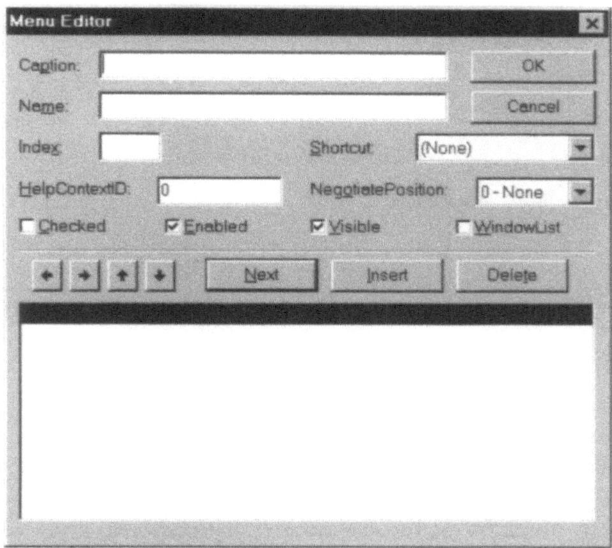

Fig. 12.4
The menu editor dialog box.

The **Caption** is the menu title item which appears on the menu bar, for example, *File*, or *Help*. As the caption is typed, it appears in the large window at the bottom of the form.

The **Name** is used to reference the menu control bar from your code. Every control needs a name.

To create the menu, type the **Caption** and **Name** for the first menu caption.

- Select **Next** to make another entry.

- Specify a new **Caption** and **Name**. If this control is a menu item, not a title item, press the right-arrowed button on the form.
- A separator bar can be created by putting a hyphen as the **Caption**.

Figure 12.5 shows the completed **Menu Design** window.

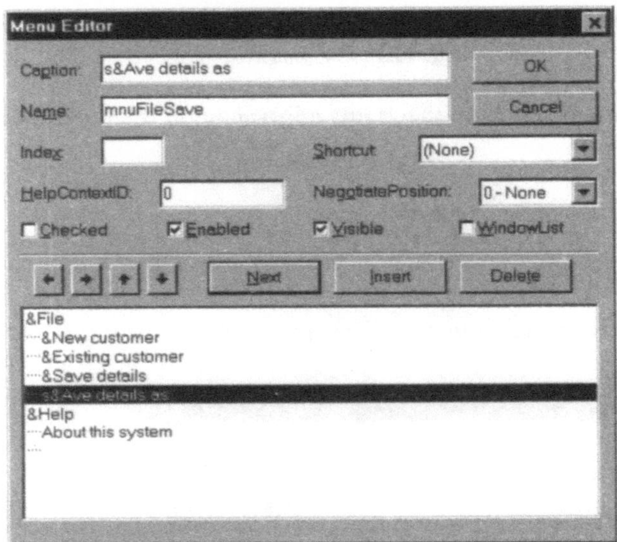

Fig. 12.5   *The completed menu.*

Amending the Menu

Visual Basic allows you easily to amend a menu:

- Open the menu editor
- Select the entry in the menu that you want to change
- Click on **Insert** to make another entry before the selected control
- Click on **Delete** to remove the selected control
- Move between the menu items by using the up and down arrow keys
- Change the level of the menu item by using the left and right arrows.

When a menu item is selected, a **Click** event occurs and Visual Basic constructs a template procedure for processing this event.

Shortcut Keys

Visual Basic allows you to specify "short-cut" keys for invoking menu elements, as shown in fig. 12.6, so that the elements can be selected from the keyboard as well as by the mouse.

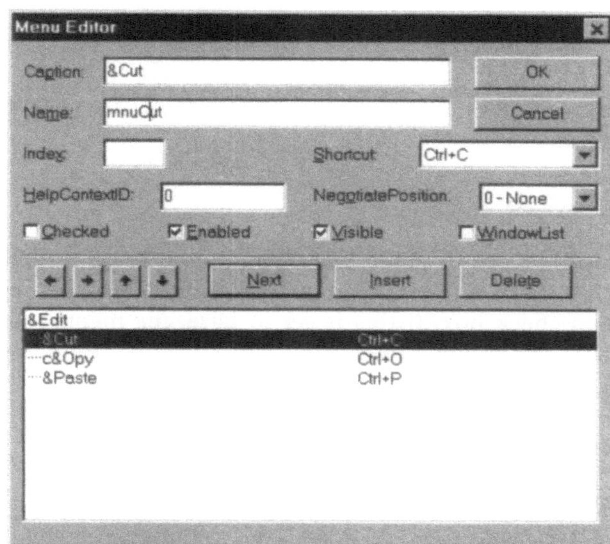

Fig. 12.6
Specifying short-cut keys.

For a pull-down menu that appears on the menu bar, for example, **File** and **Help**, the menu can be opened by pressing **Alt** with the underlined character from the menu title, for example, **Alt+F** opens the **File** menu. The character of the menu title to be underlined is indicated by the "&" character in the **Caption** field on the **Menu Design** Window, for example, "&File".

For an element on a displayed menu, that option can be executed by pressing the underlined character of the caption. As for the menu title, the character of a menu element to be underlined is indicated by the "&", for example, **E&xit** on the **File** menu can be invoked by keying that character ("x").

- Menu items can be invoked directly by setting the **ShortCut** list in the **Menu Design** window.
- The short-cut keys (fig. 12.7) are displayed on the drop-down combo.

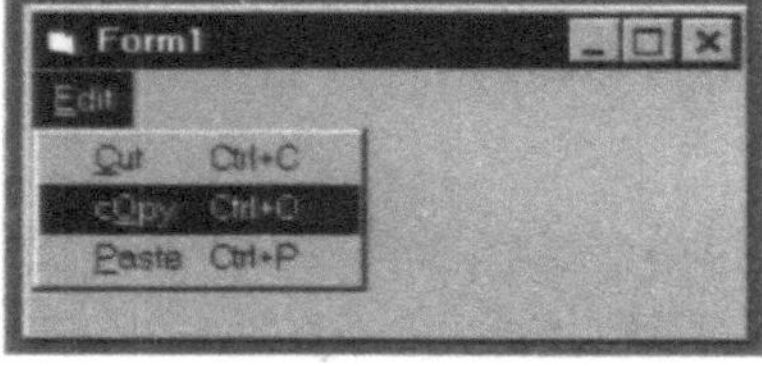

Fig. 12.7
Short-cut keys.

You can have short-cut keys that invoke menu elements directly, even when they are not being displayed. These are set from the **Shortcut** combo in the menu editor dialog. Short-cut keys are displayed on the menu to the right of the corresponding element, for example, *"Cut* **Ctrl+X**".

Short-cut keys are not limited just to menu items. An access can be created for any control that has a **Caption** property, simply by putting the "&" character in front of the character that you want to use as an access key. For example, if a button has a **Caption** of *Quit*, it can be invoked by typing **Alt+Q** if the **Caption** property is changed to *&Quit*.

Enabling and Disabling Controls

Sometimes menu controls need to be disabled, for example, the **Paste** command in an editor if nothing has been **Cut** or **Copied** beforehand. All the menu commands have an **Enabled** check box. If this is set to false, the menu control appears in light grey and does not respond to clicking. The run-time command to disable a command is:

> *Control_name.***Enabled** = *false*

- If a menu title is disabled, all the controls below it are autom .tically disabled.
- Menu controls can also be disabled by making them invisible:

> *Control_name.***Visible** = *false*

Menu Properties

Menu elements can have a check mark displayed alongside them by setting the **Checked** property:

> *Control_name.***Checked** = *true*

- The **Window** list control is used with an MDI application to indicate if the menu control displays a list of open child windows.
- The **HelpContextId** property is used to assign a unique context identifier. This is used to find the Help topic in the Help file.

13
MDI Applications

Introduction

Visual Basic allows you to create applications with many forms, however some applications require a special type of form that contains other forms. Visual Basic allows you to create such a single container form called a parent window. This is called a Multiple Document Interface or MDI.

In this chapter you will learn:

- What MDI forms are.
- How to create an MDI form and child forms.
- How to arrange forms.

Creating an MDI Application

The form shown in fig. 13.1 has two child forms within the parent form. A restriction is that only one MDI form containing all the child forms can be created in a project.

Fig. 13.1
Parent and child forms.

In order to create an MDI application:

- Create an MDI form by selecting the **MDI Form** option from the **Insert** menu.
- Create child forms by selecting the **Form** option from the **Insert** menu.
- Change the **MDIChild** property of the child forms to true.
- When you run your application, the MDI form is automatically displayed.
- Use the **Hide** and **Show** methods to control which child menus are displayed.

You can only have one MDI form per application. After one MDI form has been created, the **MDI Form** option on the **Insert** menu is greyed, indicating that it is unavailable. MDI forms do not have the **MDIChild** property.

At design-time, child forms behave like any other form – they are not restricted to the area inside the MDI form.

At run-time, all child forms are displayed within the MDI form, but they can be moved and sized within this area as normal. Both child and parent forms can be minimised, but when a parent form is minimised, it and all the child forms it contains are represented by a single icon.

Arranging Forms

Child forms can be displayed in a variety of ways using the **Arrange** method (fig. 13.2).

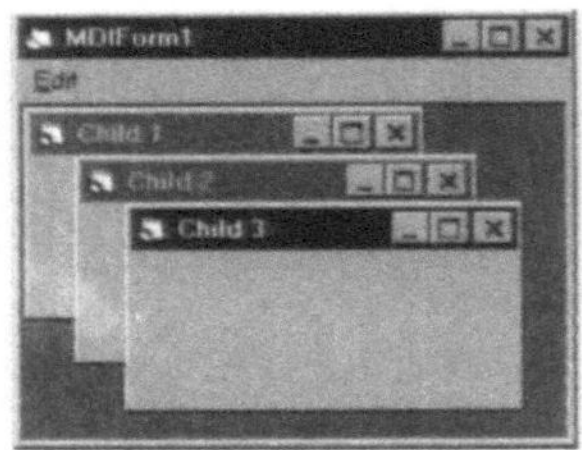

MdiForm1.**Arrange**
vbCascade

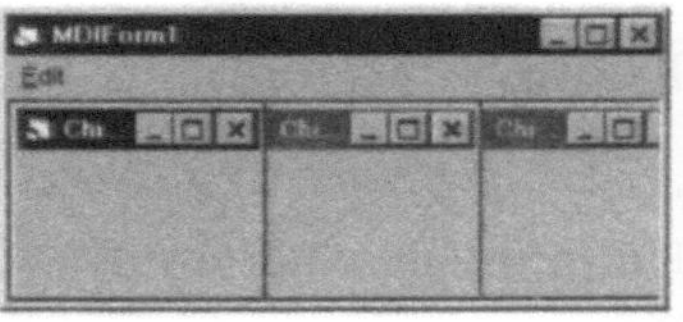

MdiForm1.**Arrange**
vbTileVertical

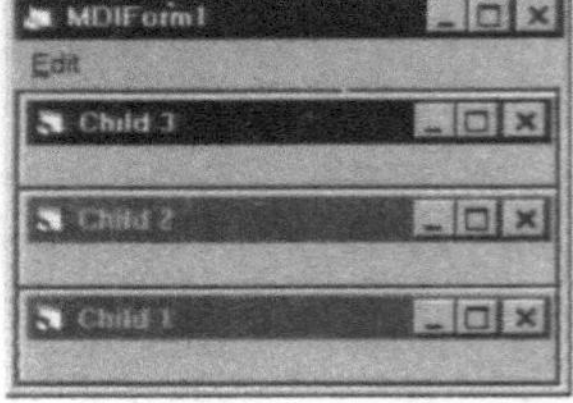

MdiForm1.**Arrange**
vbTileHorizontal

Fig. 13.2   *Arranging child forms.*

Icons can also be arranged by:

MdiForm1.Arrange vbArrangeIcons

The Start-up Form

If you only have one form in your application, this will be displayed when it runs. If you have more than one form, you need to specify the form that first appears when it is run:

- Select the **Tools** menu

- Select **Options.**
- Select the **Project** page.
- Set the **Start-up Form** option to the chosen form.

Modal and Non-Modal Forms

When displaying forms, Visual Basic needs to know if the form is modal or not. A modal form is one that requires the user to take some action before the focus can switch to another form.

A non-modal form allows the user to switch the focus before taking any action.

Loading and Unloading Forms

Visual Basic provides a set of simple commands for controlling which form is displayed.

The **Load** statement loads a form into memory:

Load Formname

Load does not display the form but makes it available for display.

Forms can be unloaded using the **Unload** statement:

Unload Formname

The **Show** method displays a loaded form:

*Formname.**Show** Modestyle*

- *Modestyle* is an optional parameter. If a value of **vbModal** (0) is specified, the form is modal.
- If the *Modestyle* is **vbModeless** (1), the form is non-modal. This is the default.

If you have not loaded a form into memory before using the **Show** method, Visual Basic automatically loads the form. The only reason for using **Load** is to improve the speed of the software; the form can be loaded into memory before it is required. This is a relatively slow process since the form will be stored on disk. If it is in memory and the **Show** method is used, the form will appear much faster.

The Hide Method

The **Hide** method is the opposite of the **Show** method and makes a form invisible:

*Formname.**Hide***

- The **Hide** method sets the visible property of the form to false.
- **Hide** does not unload a form from memory.
- **Hide** preserves the run-time properties of the form, while **Unload** does not.

14

Grid Control

Introduction

There is often a need to display information in the form of tables. Visual Basic provides the grid control to allow you to do this easily.

In this chapter you will learn how to:

- Create grids.
- Control grid cells.
- Format grids.

Installing the Grid Control

By default, the **Grid** control will not be installed in your application. This is a custom control which is a separate file GRID32.OCX. In order to install it, select the **Custom Controls** option from the **Tools** menu.

The custom controls dialog is shown in fig. 14.1.

Select the **Microsoft Grid Control** option.

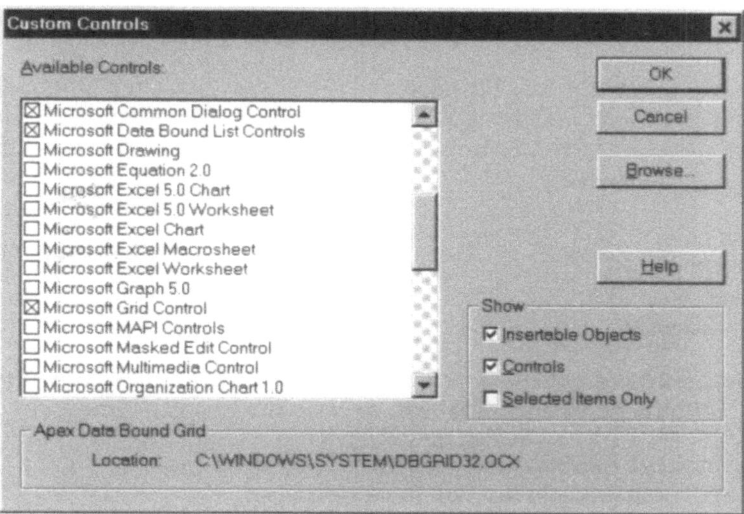

Fig. 14.1   *Installing the grid control.*

The **Grid** control will now be displayed in the toolbox, as shown in fig 14.2.

Fig. 14.2   *The **Grid** control.*

Creating a Grid

The **Grid** control (fig. 14.3) allows the application to display information in rows and columns:

- Each cell in the grid can be controlled separately
- Rows can be added and deleted at run-time
- Columns can be added and deleted at run-time.

A grid is created by selecting the **Grid** control and clicking the mouse in the place where you want to insert it.

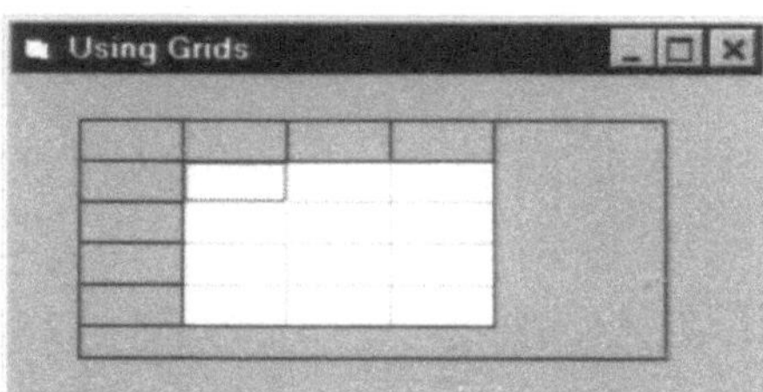

Fig. 14.3
*Using the **Grid** control.*

Grid Properties

There are two types of grid cells: fixed and non-fixed. The fixed type is shaded in grey and fixed cells do not scroll. A non-fixed area is able to scroll. If you want to adjust the number of fixed or non-fixed columns and rows, you need to change the following properties:

- **Rows.**
- **Columns.**
- **FixedRows.**
- **FixedColumns.**

To change the height of a row or the width of a column, change the **RowHeight** and the **ColWidth** properties. This can only be done at run-time.

- The number of the first row and column is zero.
- The (0,0) cell is in the top left of the grid.

The dimensions of the grid are usually specified in the form load procedure:

```
Private Sub Form_Load ()
    Grid1.Rows = 6
    Grid1.Cols = 6
End Sub
```

Writing to the Grid

There are some restrictions on setting and changing the contents of grids. Cells cannot be written to at design-time, and at run-time users can select the grid but cannot manipulate the text in it. Text is usually loaded into the grid in the **Form_Load** subroutine by setting the **Text** property (fig. 14.4) of the currently active cell, which is indicated by the current values assigned to the **Cols** and **Rows** properties.

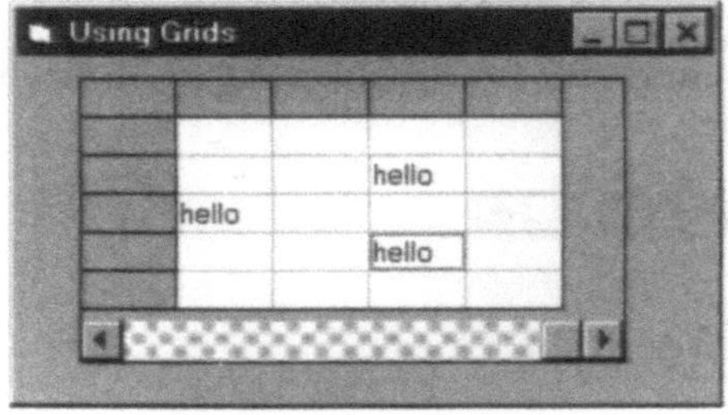

Fig. 14.4
The **Text property of grids.**

```
Private Sub Grid1_Click
    Grid1.Text = "hello"
End Sub
```

In the example above, you activate a cell by clicking on it and the word *"hello"* appears in the selected cell. Note that vertical and horizontal scroll bars appear if the size of the grid is not big enough to display all of the rows and columns.

Selecting Cells

When a cell has been selected the **CellSelected** property is set to true, otherwise it is set to false. This property is only available at run-time not design-time.

[form.]grid.CellSelected

Sometimes it is useful to select an area. The selected area is defined by four properties which specify the limits of the selected area. These properties are:

- **SelEndCol.**
- **SelStartCol.**
- **SelEndRow.**
- **SelStartRow.**

The next example selects the cells specified, and if the mouse is clicked within the selected area prints "Yes"; otherwise it prints "No". The selected area is shown in a different colour from that of unselected cells. It can be determined whether or not a cell has been selected by referring to the **CellSelected** property:

```
Private Sub Grid1_Click ()
    Grid1.SelStartCol = 2
    Grid1.SelEndCol = 4
    Grid1.SelStartRow = 3
    Grid1.SelEndRow = 5
    If Grid1.CellSelected = true Then
        Grid1.Text = "Yes"
        Else Grid1.Text = "No"
    End If
End Sub
```

The effects of this code are shown in fig. 14.5.

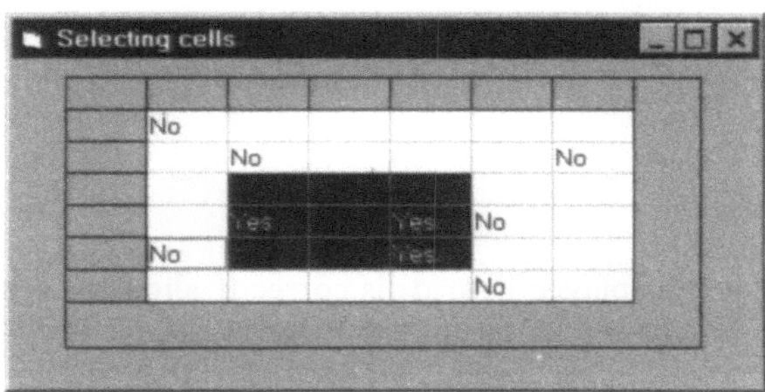

Fig. 14.5
Selecting cells.

Note: Many cells can be selected, but only one cell can be active – this is the cell specified by the **Row** and **Col** properties. An active cell need not be selected. Selected cells are highlighted, while the active cell has a dotted border.

Adding and Removing Rows

You can add new rows at run-time using:

*Grid.**Additem** item [,index]*

- Item specifies the contents of the first cell in the new row.

To specify the contents of more than one cell along a row, separate the cell contents by tabs:

*Grid1.**Additem** "one"&Chr$(9) & "two"&Chr$(9) & "three"*

- The value of index specifies the position of the new row.
- You cannot use **Additem** with fixed rows.
- The **Additem** method actually creates a new row – it does not simply put text into an existing row.

You can also remove rows at run-time using:

*Grid.**RemoveItem** index*

- The value of index specifies the number of the row to be removed.
- You cannot use **RemoveItem** with fixed rows.

ColWidth and RowWidth Properties

The **ColWidth** property determines the width of the column, for example

*Grid1.**Colwidth**(2) = 2000*

assigns to the second column the width of 2000 twips; while

*Grid1.**RowWidth**(3) = 1000*

assigns the width of the third row to 1000 twips. This property can be used at run-time.

Aligning Text

It is important that the text displayed in grids is correctly aligned so that it looks clear. Text in cells can be aligned using the **ColAlignment** and the **FixedAlignment** properties.

- The **FixedAlignment** property specifies the type of alignment for fixed cells and **ColAlignment** for all other cells. For example:

  *Grid1.**FixedAlignment**(column_number) = Alignment_Type*

- The value of the *Alignment_Type* determines the type of alignment.

Value of Alignment_Type	Meaning
0	Left justified
1	Right justified
2	Centred

The default is left justified.

Scroll Bars

Scroll bars can be displayed to enable a large grid to be viewed by using the **ScrollBars** property:

*Grid1.**ScrollBars** = 2*

Value of ScrollBars	Meaning
0	No scroll bars.
1	Horizontal scroll bars.
2	Vertical scroll bars.
3	Horizontal and vertical scroll bars.

The default is for both horizontal and vertical scroll bars.

Adding Text to Grids

Unlike most other parts of Visual Basic, some aspects of using grids are not intuitive; in this respect, grids are one of the more tricky aspects of Visual Basic. Writing text to grid cells often causes problems, and it is worth noting the following key points:

- You cannot write any text to fixed cells.
- In order to add headings to these sections, you need to make them non-fixed using the statements:

Grid1.FixedCols = 0
Grid1.FixedRows = 0

- Write the text to them, using statements of the form:

Grid1.Row = 0
Grid1.Col = 0
Grid1.Text = "hello world"

Confusing Row and Rows

Another source of problems in this area is confusion between the **Row** and **Rows** properties and the **Col** and **Cols** property:

- The **Row** and Col properties indicate the current cell in the grid.
- The **Rows** and **Cols** properties indicate the current number of rows and columns in the grid.

Rows and columns are numbered from zero upwards, so the number of the last row in a grid in which **Row** = 5 is 4.
The **Rows** and **Cols** properties can be changed dynamically at run-time.

Editing Cell Contents

If you want to allow the user to amend the contents of a cell by typing in that cell, there is a major problem since Visual Basic does not allow this. However, there is a clumsy way around this:

- Create a text control (which does accept input at run-time) and make it invisible.
- When the user clicks on a cell, the click event processing routine transfers the focus to the text box, makes it visible and positions it so that it fits exactly over the cell.
- It requires some tedious but straightforward arithmetic to make sure that the text box is exactly the same size as the grid cell.
- Most people write a subroutine to do this, as it is a common operation if you are frequently working with grids.
- When the user types return, the contents of the text box are transferred to the grid cell and the text box is made invisible.

15
Creating Graphics

Introduction

Graphics are a key feature of many Windows programs, and Visual Basic provides a good set of tools for incorporating and manipulating graphics and even for creating simple graphics.

In this chapter you will learn about:

- Graphical controls.
- Graphics methods.
- The co-ordinate system.
- The **Image** control.
- The **Picture** control.
- The **Stretch** property.
- The **AutoSize** property.
- Adding a picture at run-time.
- The **Line** and **Circle** methods.
- Drawing basic shapes.
- Drawing arcs and pie charts.

Use of Graphics

Graphics can be added and created both at design-time and run-time. Visual Basic offers only a simple set of graphical controls for creating graphics, but you need to use a drawing package such as CorelDraw to produce Windows Metafiles which have a .WMF extension or bit-mapped (BMP) files. Visual Basic offers two ways of handling graphics:

- Graphical controls
- Graphics methods – by writing code.

The terms graphical controls and graphics methods are used as they reflect the terminology used in the *Microsoft Visual Basic Programmers Guide*. I think that they are confusing terms!

The Co-ordinate System

One of the major benefits of Visual Basic is that the positioning of controls is done by dragging. However, in some circumstances, it may be necessary to control the position of a graphic at run-time, for example, to create the impression of animation. In order to do this, it is important to understand the co-ordinate system (fig. 15.1) used by Visual Basic

The unit used is the twip. 567 twips = 1 cm or 1440 inches. Twip stands for twentieth of a point. The top left of the screen is the 0,0 position.

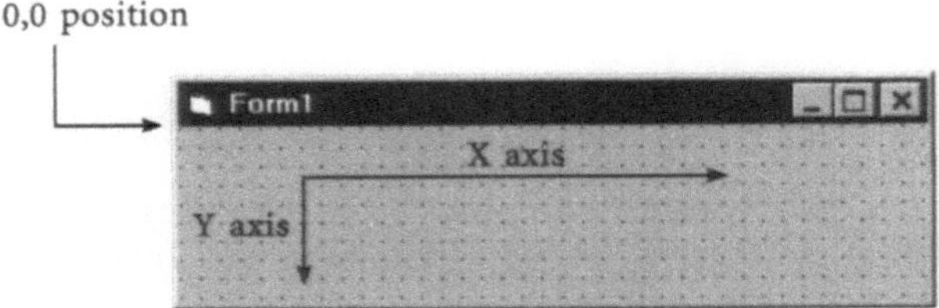

Fig. 15.1   *The co-ordinate system.*

- The **Left** property refers to the co-ordinate of the left side of a control.
- The **Top** property refers to the co-ordinate of the top of the control.

The twip refers to the size when the image is printed. The size on the screen is dependent on the size and type of the monitor.

Note: The co-ordinate frame used is that of the container. If the image is on a form, it is the form's co-ordinate system that is used.

The position and size of the current control (fig. 15.2) are displayed on the left of the toolbar in the default units of twips.

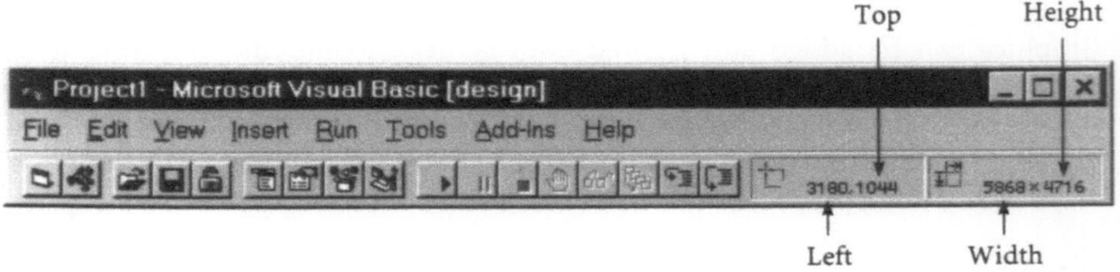

Fig. 15.2   *The position and size of the current control.*

The Image Control

The **Image** control (fig. 15.3) is used to incorporate existing graphics into the application. The image file must be one of the following types:

Format	Comments
Bit map	File extension BMP.
Icon	File extension ICO. A special type of bit map with a maximum size of 32 by 32 pixels.
Metafile	File extension WMF. These files are usually smaller than bit maps since the images are defined as a series of lines and basic shapes.

Fig. 15.3 The **Image** control.

- Click on the **Image** control to select it.
- Move the cursor onto the screen and press the left button. This fixes one corner of the box that delimits the graphic.
- Drag using the mouse to the position of the opposite corner and release.
- Select the file containing the graphic.

The file containing the graphic is specified in the properties box by the **Picture** property. By selecting this property and double clicking, you can browse through the directories on your disks and select the file containing the graphic.

The Stretch Property

This is a property of **Image** controls only. The default value for the **Stretch** property is false. When an image is imported, the **Image** control resizes itself to fit the image. If the image control is resized, the image remains the same size. However, if **Stretch** is true, the image resizes itself so that it fits the size of the image control. The screen in fig. 15.4 shows the same images in three differently sized image controls.

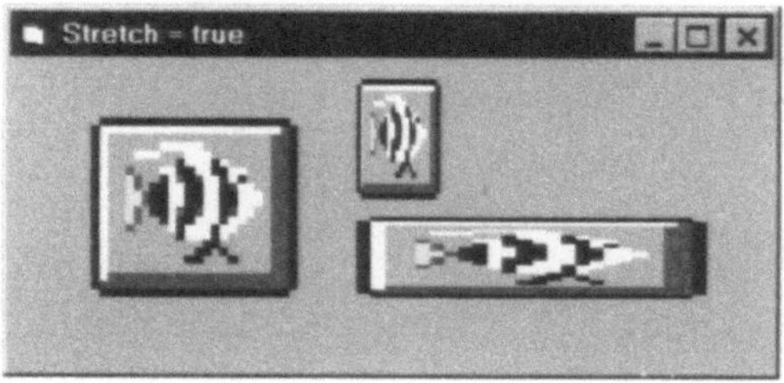

Fig. 15.4
The **Stretch** property.

Clipboard Images

Images can also be added to the application from the clipboard by:

- Pasting an image to the clipboard from another application, such as CorelDraw
- Returning to Visual Basic
- Selecting a Picture box, **Image** control or a Form – they all have a **Picture** property
- Selecting **Paste** from the **Edit** Menu.

The PictureBox Control

Fig. 15.5   *The **PictureBox** control.*

The same sequence of operations is required to use Picture boxes.

- Click on the **PictureBox** control to select it.
- Move the cursor onto the screen and press the left button. This fixes one corner of the box which delimits the graphic.
- Drag the mouse to the position of the opposite corner and release.
- Select the file containing the graphic.

The AutoSize Property

An especially useful property of picture boxes is the **AutoSize** property (fig. 15.6).

When **AutoSize** = true, the control automatically resizes to fit the picture.

When **AutoSize** = false, the picture is not re-scaled to fit the size of the picture box – if the picture box is shrunk, the portion of the image displayed is reduced, as shown in fig. 15.6.

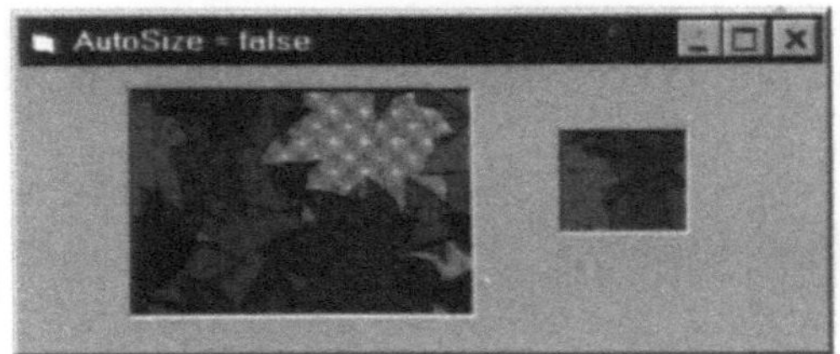

Fig. 15.6
*The **AutoSize** property.*

The Image and Picture Box Controls

Image controls and **PictureBox** controls are very similar, but there are several important differences:

- Image boxes do not have the **AutoSize** property, but they automatically resize to fit the image.
- Image controls have the **Stretch** property.
- If you simply want to display a picture, the **Image** control is the best choice, since this control uses fewer system resources than a picture box.
- **Image** controls can only contain pictures. They cannot contain other controls or run-time graphics.

Adding a Picture at Run-Time

At run-time, pictures can be added by:

- The **LoadPicture** function
- Copying a picture from one object to another.

The **LoadPicture** function has the following form:

*Shape1.**Picture** = **LoadPicture**("D:\IMAGES\ARROW.BMP")*

This replaces the existing image.
Pictures can be erased by:

*Shape1.**Picture** = **LoadPicture**("")*

Pictures can be copied using normal assignment statements:

*Shape1.**Picture** = Shape2.**Picture***

This also replaces the existing picture.
There is a trade-off between including pictures in the design and loading them at run-time. Including pictures in the EXE file make the file larger and it takes longer to load, thus delaying the time until there can be a response on the screen. If pictures are loaded at run-time, there is a quicker response to the user on the screen but you must ensure that the pictures are distributed with the application, and the application knows in which directory the pictures are kept.

Using Graphics Methods

The graphics methods allows you to:

- Clear all graphics.
- Set and determine the colour value of a specified pixel.
- Draw lines and circles.
- Write text.

Method	Description
Cls	Clear all graphics.
PSet	Set the colour of an individual pixel.
Point	Return the colour of a pixel.
Line	Draw a line, rectangle or filled-in box.
Circle	Draw a circle, ellipse or arc.

The arguments for the co-ordinates are single precision in these methods, not integer.

Controlling Individual Pixels

[object.]PSet(x; y)[,colour]

For example:

Form1.Pset (70,50) , (127, 0, 255)
[object.]Point(x, y)

and

Point1 = Point(20.5,307.4)

If the colour argument is not used with **PSet**, the pixel is assigned the foreground colour (**ForeColor**). For all of these methods, if the object argument is not specified, the current object is used. The way in which colour is specified is dealt with later in this chapter.

Graphical Controls

There are three controls for creating graphical effects in an application:

- The **Shape** control draws a range of simple shapes, including rectangles and circles.
- The **Line** control draws lines.
- The **Image** control incorporates existing images.

All of the controls can be duplicated by using graphical methods. These three controls can only be used to create graphics at design-time. There are two advantages to using the controls over using graphical methods to produce graphics:

- Less code is required.
- The controls are optimised and use the minimum systems resources to create the graphic.

While the action of all the controls can be duplicated by using graphical methods, the reverse is not true and there are a few limitations associated with the controls.

The Line Control

Fig. 15.7 *The **Line** control.*

- Click on the **Line** control (fig. 15.7) to select it.
- Move the cursor onto the screen and press the left button. This fixes the position of one end of the line.
- Drag the mouse to the position of the other end and release.
- Amend the properties using the properties box.

A **Line** control- is a straight-line segment. The properties of the line can be controlled using the properties box to change the style of the line, its colour, and its thickness and position. The position of the line can be moved in the usual manner by selecting it and dragging. The line can be scaled by selecting it and dragging on one of the handles.

Properties of the Line Control

Property	Description
BorderColor	The colour of the drawn line.
BorderStyle	The style of the line, for example, dotted.
BorderWidth	The thickness of the line: 1 is the minimum; 8192 the maximum.
DrawMode	The colour of the line is dependent on **BorderColor** and also the colour being drawn on.
Name	The name of the control.
Visible	If set to true, the line is displayed.
X1	The horizontal co-ordinates of the start of the line.
X2	The horizontal co-ordinates of the end of the line.
Y1	The vertical co-ordinates of the start of the line.
Y2	The vertical co-ordinates of the end of the line.

The **DrawMode** property is an integer between 0 and 15. Depending on its value, various operators are applied. For example, if **DrawMode** is set to 6 the **Not** operator is applied to the colour code of the pixel being drawn on, giving the "opposite" colour.

The Shape Control

The **Shape** control (fig. 15.8) can assume a variety of pre-defined shapes:

- Rectangle (with square or rounded corners)
- Square (with square or rounded corners)

- Oval
- Circle.

Fig. 15.8   *The **Shape** control.*

The default shape is the rectangle, but other shapes can be selected by using the property box (fig. 15.9) to choose one of the available shapes.

- The colour and aspect ratios of the shape can be controlled using the properties box.
- If a circle is chosen, it is the largest circle that fits within the box delimiting the shape.
- Circles cannot be stretched into ovals.

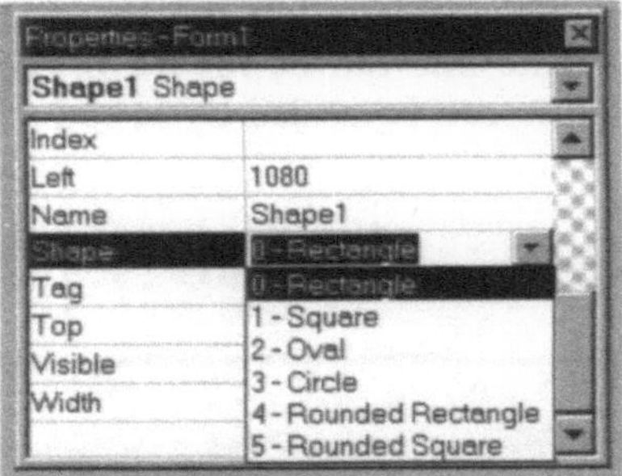

Fig. 15.9
*The **Shape** property of the **Shape** control.*

Properties of the Shape Control

The **Shape** control shares many properties with other controls, such as **Name**, **Left**, **Top**, **Height** and **Width**. In addition it has four border properties:

Property	Description
BackColor	The colour of the enclosed area of the shape.
BackStyle	If set to 0, the shape is transparent. If set to 1, the default, the shape is opaque.
FillColor	The colour of hatching drawn over the background colour.
FillStyle	How the hatching is applied.

If the **BackStyle** property indicates that the shape is transparent, the **BackColor** property is irrelevant.

The Fill Style Property

The **FillStyle** property determines how a shape is filled.

Value	Description
0	Solid fill.
1	Transparent.
2	Horizontal lines.
3	Vertical lines.
4	Diagonals up to the left.
5	Diagonals down to the left.
6	Cross-hatched with horizontal and vertical lines.
7	Cross-hatched with diagonal lines.

Drawing Lines

The **Line** control draws a line between two specified points:

[object.]Line[(x1, y1)]-(x2, y2)[,colour]

- If the object is not specified, the current object is used.
- This example draws a line between the co-ordinates specified.

Form1.Line(100,200)-(300,300)
Line -(400,400)

- The first pair of co-ordinates is optional; if they are omitted, the current position is used in place of the missing co-ordinates.

The code shown below draws the form shown in fig. 15.10:

```
Private Sub Command1_Click ( )
For x = 600 To 6600 Step 100
    Line (3600, 0)-(x, 4000)
Next x
End Sub
```

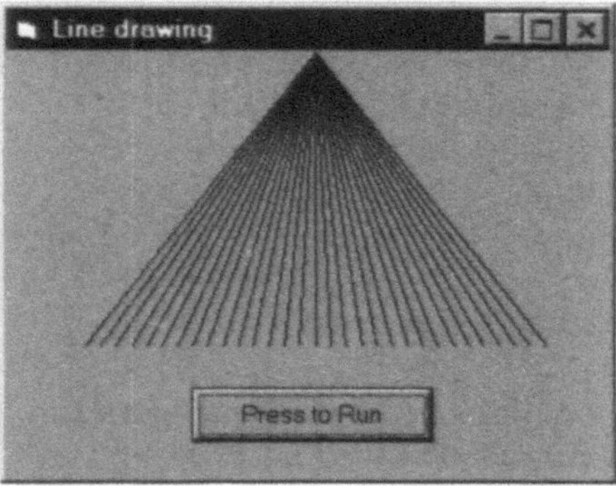

Fig. 15.10
Drawing lines.

The **Step** keyword indicates that the following co-ordinates are relative to the current position:

Line (200, 300) - (400,100) is equivalent to *Line(200,300) - Step(200, -200)*

A rectangle of side 50 is drawn using the example below:

Line (100,100) - Step(50, 0)
Line - Step(0,50)
Line - Step(-50,0)
Line - Step(0,-50)

Drawing Boxes

Stick and filled boxes are drawn using the **Line** statement by using the **B** parameter:

Line(100, 100) - Step(150, 150) , , B

This statement draws a rectangle. The first co-ordinates are the upper left corner and the second the bottom right.
The box can be filled using the **F** parameter after the **B:**

Line(100, 100) - Step(150, 150) , , BF

A stick box has an outline only. A filled box has a colour and hides whatever it sits on.

Drawing Circles

The **Circle** method draws:

- Circles.
- Ellipses.
- Arcs.
- Pie-shaped wedges.

To draw a circle, the form of the **Circle** method used is:

[object.]Circle [Step](x, y),radius [,colour]
Circle(500,200), 100

- *x* and *y* are the co-ordinates of the centre.

The **Step** keyword is optional. If this is used, it has the effect of making the co-ordinates relative to the current position.

Drawing Ellipses

[object.]Circle [Step] (x, y), radius, [colour],[start],[end],[aspect]

The key difference between drawing circles and ellipses is the aspect parameter which is the ratio of the vertical to horizontal dimensions. The aspect ratio must be a positive floating point number.

Circle (500,500), 200, , , , 3

- The start and end parameters are used in drawing arcs, but if they are omitted, commas must be used to indicate this.
- The radius is in terms of horizontal units.
- If you want to fill in the ellipse, the **FillStyle** property must be used.

The program example below draws an ellipse (fig. 15.11):

```
Private Sub Command1_Click ( )
    FillStyle = 0
    Circle (1000, 1000), 750, , , , .25
    FillStyle = 1
    Circle (4000, 1000), 500, , , , 2
End Sub
```

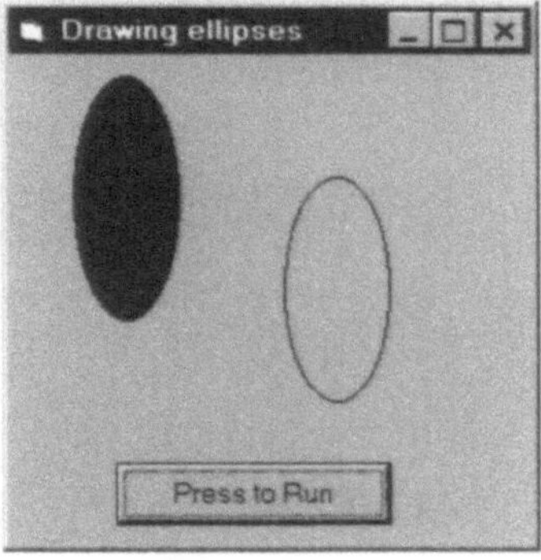

Fig. 15.11
Using the **Circle** method to draw ellipses.

The **Circle** method can also be used to draw arcs

[object.]Circle [Step] (x, y), radius, [colour],[start],[end],[aspect]

- The start and end parameters are used.
- These are specified in terms of radians

2π radians = 360 degrees.

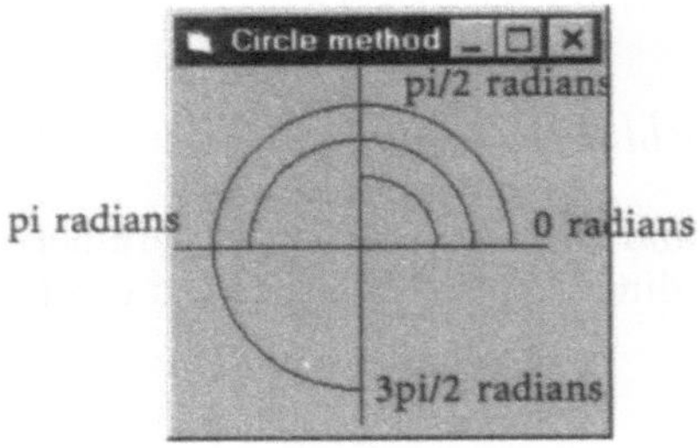

Fig. 15.12   The **Circle** method.

Fig. 15.13   Drawing a $\frac{1}{4}$ circle.

Arcs are always drawn in an anticlockwise direction, as shown in fig. 15.12. This example draws a quarter circle, as shown in fig. 15.13.

```
Private Sub Arc1 ( )
     Const PI = 3.142
     Circle(1000,1000), 500, , PI/2, PI
End Sub
```

To specify that the other three-quarters of the circle are drawn, just reverse the order of the starting and finishing parameters:

```
Private Sub Arc1 ( )
     Const PI = 3.142
     Circle(1000,1000), 500, , PI, PI/2
End Sub
```

The result of this code is shown in fig. 15.14.

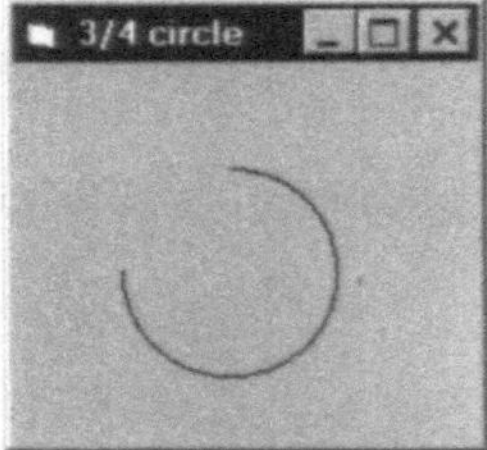

Fig. 15.14   Drawing $\frac{3}{4}$ circle.

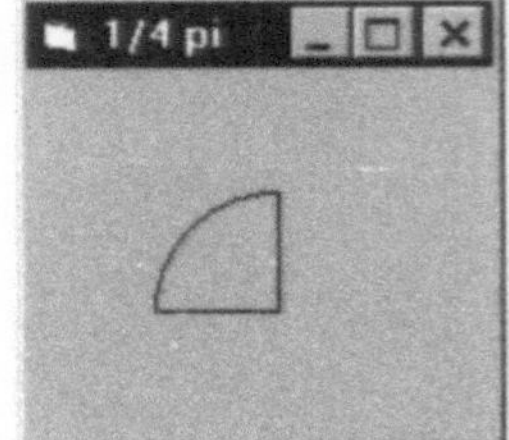

Fig. 15.15   Drawing pie shapes.

The **Circle** method can also be used to draw pie charts. If a start or end point has a negative sign, a line is added between the point and the centre of the ellipse, as shown in fig. 15.15.

```
Private Sub Arc1 ( )
     Const PI = 3.142
     Circle(1000,1000), 500, , -PI/2, -PI
End Sub
```

Changing Units

Twips are not always a convenient unit to use; fortunately the **ScaleMode** property of shapes allows you to choose either your own scaling units or a wide range of possible units.

ScaleMode Setting	Description
0	User defined.
1	Twips – the default. 1440 twips = 1 inch.
2	Points – 72 points = 1 inch.
3	Pixels.
4	Characters. When printed, a character is 1/16 inch high and 1/12 inch wide.
5	Inches.
6	Millimetres.
7	Centimetres.

If you set **ScaleMode** to zero, you need to set the limits of your working area using the properties:

- **ScaleLeft**
- **ScaleTop**
- **ScaleWidth**
- **ScaleHeight**.

If you set any of these properties, the **ScaleMode** is automatically set to zero.

Using Colours

- The foreground colour is the colour of drawn objects, such as lines and squares.
- The background colour is the colour of the background on which objects are drawn.
- A VGA screen can display 256 colours simultaneously and over 16 million different colours.
- It is a lot quicker to colour objects and backgrounds using the foreground and background concepts rather that by controlling the 300,000 pixels on the screen individually.

There are only three practical ways of controlling screen colours.

The QBColor Function

Visual Basic has 16 colours which are pre-defined. This is mainly for compatibility with earlier versions of Basic. These colours can be specified using the **QBColor** function:

QBColor (Value)

- *Value* is a integer value between 0 and 16.

Value	Colour
0	Black
1	Blue
2	Green
3	Cyan
4	Red
5	Magenta
6	Yellow
7	White
8	Grey
9	Light blue
10	Light green
11	Light cyan
12	Light red
13	Light magenta
14	Light yellow
15	Light white

The RGB Function

Screen colours can be specified in their red, green and blue components using the **RGB** function:

RGB (red, green, blue)

- *red* is the intensity of the red component.
- *green* is the intensity of the green component.
- *blue* if the intensity of the blue component.

The intensity is expressed as a value between 0 and 255. A low value indicates a low intensity.

Assigning Colours Directly

The background colour and foreground colour are represented in Visual Basic by a hexadecimal number, for example:

*Form1.**Forecolor** = &HFF0088&*
*Form1.**BackColor** = &H00FF00&*

The &H before the number indicates that it is a hexadecimal (base 16) number. A range of eight colours have been assigned. The common convention of putting 0x before a number, to indicate that it is hexadecimal, is used in this table of symbolic colour names.

Symbolic Name	Hexadecimal Value
vbBlack	0x0
vbRed	0xFF
vbGreen	0xFF00
vbYellow	0xFFFF
vbBlue	0xFF0000
vbMagenta	0xFF00FF
vbCyan	0xFFFF00
vbWhite	0xFFFFFF

A range of colours can be selected by choosing the **Color Palette** from the **View** menu.

16

Displaying and Printing

Introduction

Visual Basic provides a comprehensive set of tools for formatting information which is to be printed to the screen or to a printer.

In this chapter you will learn about:

- Putting information onto the screen and printer.
- Controlling text font and size.
- Controlling the position of information displayed.

Message Boxes, Text Boxes and Labels

The two most common ways of displaying information are to use message boxes and labels. Message boxes are used for temporary information display and appear as a dialog box. While the contents of message boxes can be controlled at run-time, the text in a label can only be controlled at design-time.

Text boxes can be used to display large amounts of information and can be changed at run-time.

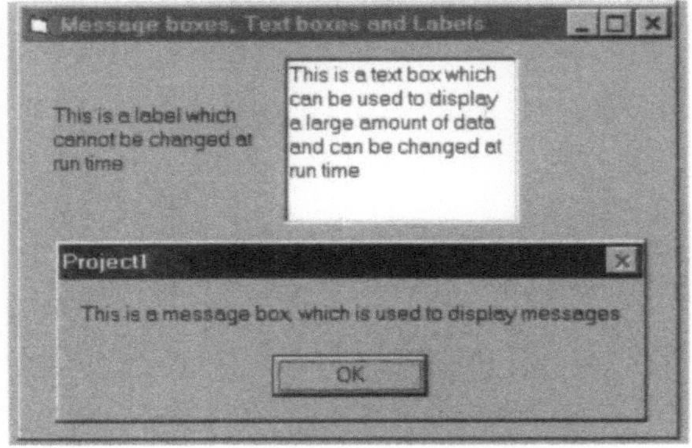

Fig. 16.1
Message boxes, text boxes and labels.

Message boxes, text boxes and labels (fig. 16.1) have already been dealt with in detail.

Controlling Fonts and Font Characteristics

Textual attributes of labels and text boxes affect all the text. It is not possible to make only part of the text bold.

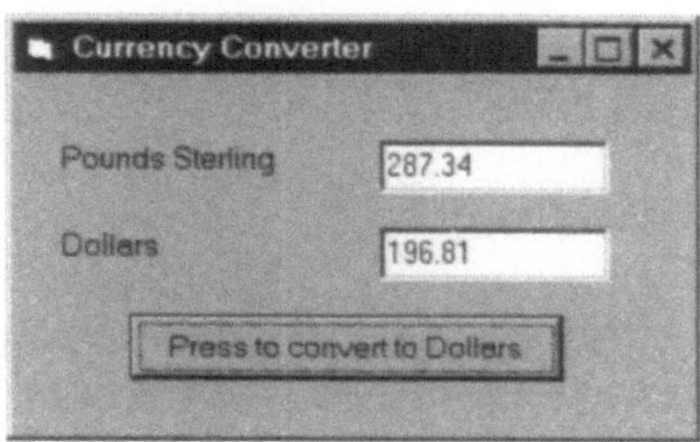

Fig. 16.2
The pounds to dollars converter.

In fig. 16.2 there are two **Label** controls with captions of *Pounds Sterling* and *Dollars*. You enter a value in the text box adjacent to the *Pounds Sterling* caption. When the button is clicked, the equivalent number of dollars is shown in the text box adjacent to the *Dollars* label.

You can display text on a form by setting the **Font** property for each of the controls of the form; however these characteristics control all the text – you cannot, for example, make part of the text italic.

Property	Type
FontName	string
FontSize	integer – in points
FontBold	boolean
FontItalic	boolean
FontStrikethru	boolean
FontUnderline	boolean
FontTransparent	boolean

Since not all properties are supported by all fonts it is advisable to set the **FontName** property first.

Using the Print Method

Visual Basic also allow you to display information anywhere on the form using the **Print** method. Print places text at the current position of the cursor and in the current font and size (but see fig. 16.3). For example:

```
Private Sub Form_Click ()
    For x = 8 To 20 Step 2
        Form1.FontSize = x
        Print "Visual Basic4"
    Next x
End Sub
```

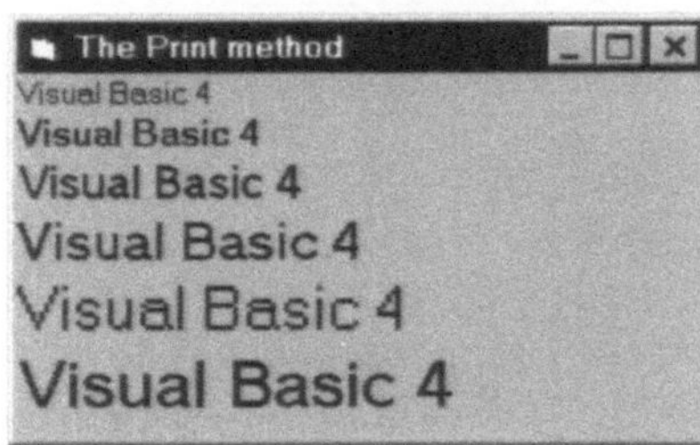

Fig. 16.3
Changing the font size.

Controlling Print Position

The **Print** method displays text at the current position given by the **CurrentX** and **CurrentY** properties measured in twips. It is recommended that you change this to a more easily understood unit – either centimetres, inches or points using the **ScaleMode** property.

The **Print** method automatically moves to a new line after printing. If you do not want this to happen, put a semicolon (;) at the end of the statement:

Another useful feature is that you can put a comma (,) after printing text. This will move to the next tab position on the line (fig. 16.4). As a default there are 14 tab positions which can be used to create 14 columns of text, provided that the text you print is not more than one column wide.

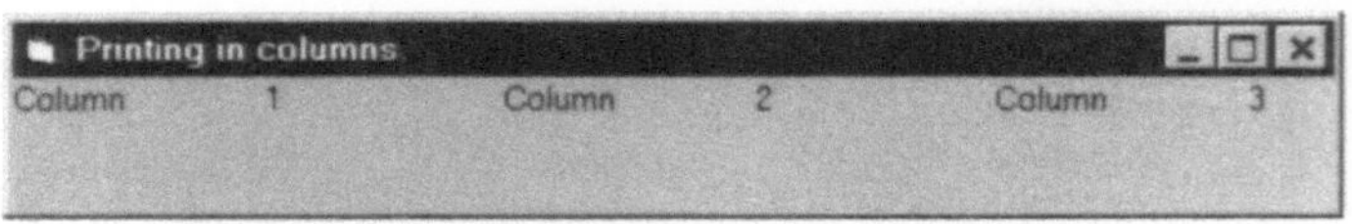

Fig. 16.4   Printing in columns.

```
Private Sub Form_Click ()
    For x = 1 To 3
        Print "Column", x,
    Next x
End Sub
```

The text is printed in three columns, but there is clearly a problem – a large unwanted gap between the word "column" and the column number. Visual Basic offers a comprehensive set of methods for allowing the user to control this and many other aspects of printing by using **Format**

Visual Basic also gives you the option of creating tab positions (fig. 16.5) by specifying column numbers:

```
Private Sub Form_Click ()
    Print Tab(10); "Name"; Tab(25); "Company";
    Print Tab(40); "Phone Number"
End Sub
```

Fig. 16.5
Using tabs.

Note the use of the semicolons to ensure that the text is printed on the same line.

Controlling Number Format

Format$ and **Format** functions allow you to specify the way in which characters are displayed;

Format[$] (expression[, fmt$])

fmt$ describes how the number (in expression) is to be formatted (fig. 16.6) when displayed.

Visual Basic supplies a number of standard formats for displaying numbers:

Number Formats	Description
general number	Numbers displayed with no thousand separator.
currency	Displays with a thousand separator; negative numbers in brackets and only two digits after the decimal point.
fixed	At least one digit before the point and two after.
standard	Similar to fixed but inserts a thousands separator.
percent	Similar to fixed but multiplies the number by 100, displays the result as a percentage and appends the percent sign (%).
scientific	Displays the number in standard scientific notation.

```
Private Sub Form_Click ()
    value = 9876543.21
    Print "The number in general format is : "; Format$(value, "general
        number")
    Print "The number in currency format is : "; Format$(value, "currency")
    Print "The number in standard format is : "; Format$(value, "standard")
    Print "The number in scientific format is : "; Format$(value, "scientific")
End Sub
```

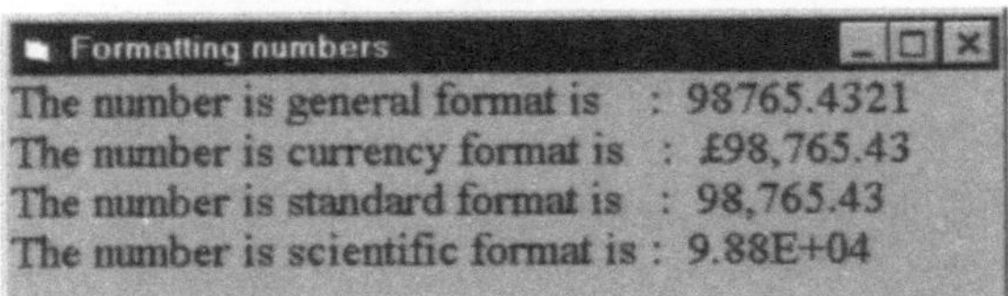

Fig. 16.6
Formatting numbers.

Boolean operators are either zero or non-zero. These can be displayed using **Format$** and the boolean operators given below:

Binary	Description
yes/no	Any non-zero value displays "Yes". A zero value displays "No".
true/false	Any non-zero value displays "false". A zero value displays "true".
on/off	Any non-zero value displays "On". A zero value displays "Off".

Custom Formats

Visual Basic also allows users to create their own formats using a set of symbols shown below:

Symbol	Description
0	Digit place holder. A leading or trailing 0 must be placed in this position if padding is necessary to fill it.
#	Digit place holder. Digits may be printed here. Leading/ trailing 0s are not displayed.
.	Decimal place holder.
,	Thousands separator.
-+$£() space	Literal characters. These characters are entered into the formatted string exactly as they appear.

For example:

Example	Result
Print Format$(876.34, "00000.0000")	00876.3400
Print Format$(876.34, "#####.####")	876.34
**Print Format$**(876.345, "$##.00")	$876.35 (to 2 dec. places)

Displaying Dates and Times

Visual Basic offers a range of standard formats for displaying dates and times (fig. 16.7) which are used with **Format[$]**.

Date Formats	Description
general date	Uses the short date and time formats, depending on the information in the expression field.
long date	Displays the entire month in textual form, for example, 1 June 1995.
medium date	The month is displayed in abbreviated textual form and the year abbreviated, for example, 1 Jun-95.
short date	The month is in number form and the year abbreviated, for example, 25/12/94.

```
Private Sub Form_Click ()
    Print "The General date format is :"; Tab(30); Format$(Now, "general
        date")
    Print "The Long date format is :"; Tab(30); Format$(Now, "long date")
    Print "The Medium date format is :"; Tab(30); Format$(Now, "medium
        date")
    Print "The Short date format is :"; Tab(30); Format$(Now, "short date")
End Sub
```

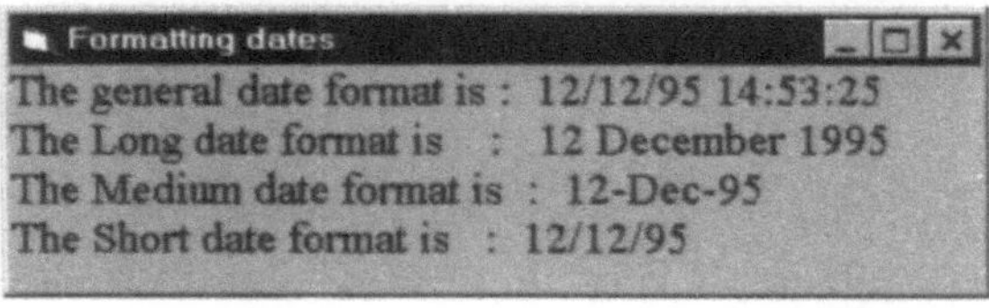

Fig. 16.7
Formatting dates.

Similarly there are a range of standard formats for printing the time (fig. 16.8):

Time Formats	Description
long time	The "international" section of the control panel describes the format used for hours, minutes and seconds and "AM" or "PM" if the 12 hour format is being used, for example, 12:15:42.
medium time	The medium time format displays the hours and seconds and either "AM" or "PM". The international setting for the hour/minute separator is used but the format of "AM" and "PM" is ignored.
short time	The short time format displays the hours and seconds separated by the international setting of the hour/minute separator.

```
Private Sub Form_Click ()
    Print "The Long time format is :"; Tab(30); Format$(Now, "long time")
    Print "The Medium time format is :"; Tab(30); Format$(Now, "medium
        time")
    Print "The Short time format is :"; Tab(30); Format$(Now, "short time")
End Sub
```

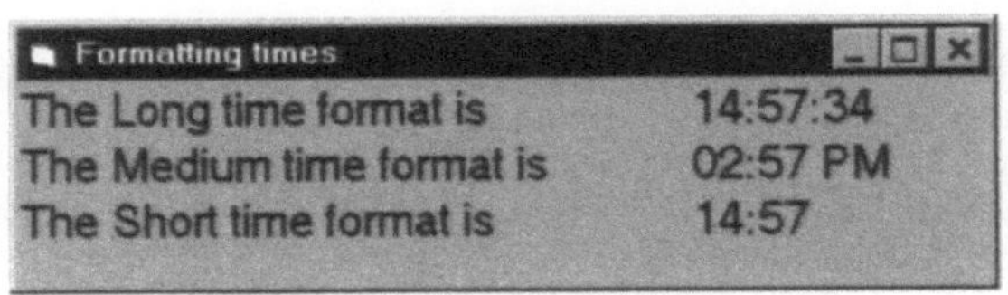

Fig. 16.8
Formatting time.

Writing to a Printer

The printer can be addressed in two ways:

- The first technique is to assemble the information on the printer object and then print the printer object.
- The second method is to assemble the information on a form and then print the form.

If you are developing a Visual Basic program for another user, you need to ensure that it has the capabilities that you are using.

The Printer Object

Visual Basic supports a drawing space called the **Printer** object which is device independent. You write to this drawing space using the **Print, Line** and all the usual methods that are used for displaying on the screen. When you are ready to print the page you have built up, you call the **NewPage** method. The page size of the **Printer** object is defined by its **Height** and **Width** properties.

Printer.NewPage

NewPage maintains page numbers that can be used for creating numbered pages; this is saved in the property **Page**. When you are ready to print out the last page, you call the **EndDoc** method; if you forget to do this, there is an automatic **EndDoc** if the **Printer** object is not empty.

The example below prints "Page number 1" on the first page and "Page number 2" on the second page, before closing the printer object:

Printer.Print "Page number " + Printer.Page
Printer.NewPage
Printer.Print "Page number " + Printer.Page
Printer.EndDoc

The PrintForm Method

The **PrintForm** method prints the specified form. If no form is specified, the form that holds the focus is printed.

*Form1.**Printform***

The **PrintForm** method relies on the application assembling the information on a form on the screen and then copying the information, pixel by pixel, to the printer. The output can be disappointing on a high-quality printer because the printer resolution, for example, 400 pixels per inch, may be much greater than the screen resolution, for example, 100 pixels per inch.

17
Mouse and Keyboard Events

Introduction

Virtually all Windows programs use the mouse. In this chapter you will learn about:

- Mouse movement.
- Mouse button pressing and releasing.
- Dragging and dropping applications.
- The effect of the **Shift, Ctrl** and **Alt** buttons on using the mouse.
- The **KeyPress** event.
- The **KeyDown** event.
- The **KeyUp** event.

Mouse Events

There are three mouse events that Visual Basic recognises:

Mouse Event	Description
MouseDown	A mouse button is pressed.
MouseUp	A pressed mouse button is released.
MouseMove	The mouse is moved from its current position.

The same **MouseUp** and **MouseDown** events occur irrespective of which mouse button is used. In order to find out which button is used, you must refer to an argument passed by Visual Basic to the event handler.

Mouse Event Arguments

The mouse events all use the same arguments:

Argument	Description
Button	A bit field in which the three least significant bits give the status of the buttons.
Shift	A bit field in which the least significant buttons give the status of the Shift, Ctrl and Alt buttons.
X, Y	Location of the mouse pointer.

The program shown below can be used to draw lines (fig. 17.1) on the form. The button which has been pressed is indicated by the first parameter. Visual Basic automatically creates the outline subroutine, including the list of parameters that are passed to that routine.

Private Sub Form_MouseDown (Button As Integer, Shift As Integer, X As Single, Y As Single)
Line - (X, Y)
End Sub

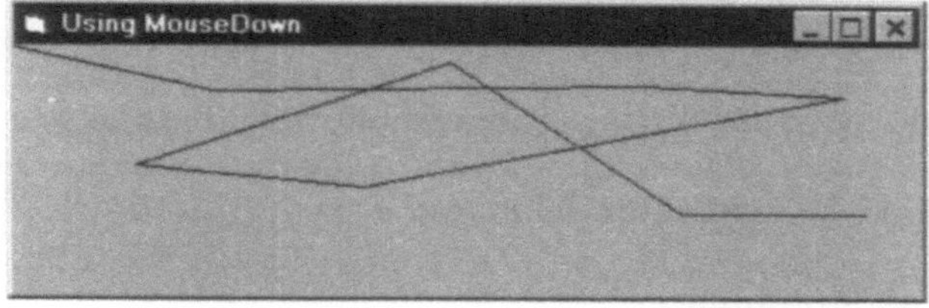

Fig. 17.1
Drawing lines.

The **Line** method is used to draw a line from the present point to the specified point. Every time the **MouseDown** event occurs, a line is drawn to the new position as shown. In this example, it does not matter which mouse button is pressed.

The Click Events

The following events are associated with the mouse buttons:

- The **Click** and **DblClick** events occur as a result of using the mouse buttons.
- The **Click** and **DblClick** events do not differentiate which mouse button has been pressed.
- The same event handler is used irrespective of which button is used.

Windows measures the time between successive clicks and therefore is able to differentiate between single and double clicks. This time period is configurable using the Windows control panel.

The MouseDown, MouseUp Events

When a mouse button is pressed, a **MouseDown** event occurs. When it is released, a **MouseUp** event occurs. The usage of these events differs from the **Click** and **DblClick** events in that they allow the programmer to determine which button has been pressed.

> *Private Sub Command1_MouseDown (Button **As Integer**, Shift **As Integer**, X **As Single**, Y **As Single**)*

These events receive as parameters a value indicating which button has been pressed and the status of the **Shift**, **Alt** and **Ctrl** keys.

The Button Argument

The **Button** parameter indicates the status of each of the three mouse buttons:

- **Button** = 001_2 (decimal 1)   The left button caused the event.
- **Button** = 010_2 (decimal 2)   The right button caused the event.
- **Button** = 100_2 (decimal 4)   The middle button caused the event.

If you press more than one button, this is treated by Visual Basic as two events. If you want to differentiate between the buttons, which all generate the same event, you need to do so by testing the value in the event handler.

The Shift, Ctrl and Alt Arguments

The **Shift** argument is used in a similar way to the Button argument:

- **Shift** = 001_2 (decimal 1)   The **Shift** button is pressed.
- **Shift** = 010_2 (decimal 2)   The **Ctrl** button is pressed.
- **Shift** = 100_2 (decimal 4)   The **Alt** button is pressed

If **Shift** = 3, both the **Shift** and the **Ctrl** buttons are pressed. If you want to take separate action depending on whether any combination of these buttons is pressed, you must test the value of the **Shift** argument in the event handler.

Dragging and Dropping

Dragging and dropping are the techniques used to move a control from one position to another using the mouse.

A control is dragged by moving the pointer onto the control and pressing the left mouse button. As the mouse is dragged, the control moves. When the button is released, the control is dropped into its new position.

Visual Basic fully supports drag and drop using one method, **Drag,** and two events, **DragOver** and **DragDrop.**

The Drag Method

The **Drag** method goes in the source code for the **MouseDown** event:

*CtrlName.**Drag** action*

The optional *action* parameter specifies the type of drag action taken:

Value	Action
0	Cancel dragging.
1	Start dragging the control.
2	Drop the control.

The default value for the action parameter is 1 (start dragging the control).
The **MouseDown** event for the control that is to be dragged and dropped must
contain a statement that allows the control to be dragged. When the mouse
button is released, the control is dropped into its new location.

```
Private Sub Picture1_MouseDown (Button As Integer, Shift As Integer, x As
Single, y As Single)
     Picture1.Drag 1          'this starts dragging the control
End Sub

Private Sub Picture1_MouseUp (Button As Integer, Shift As Integer, x As
Single, y As Single)
     Picture1.Drag 2          'this drops the control
End Sub
```

The form must be prepared to respond to the dropping of the control by using
the **DragDrop** event. If you do not do this, you will be able to drag the control but
when you release the button to drop the dragged control, it will return to its
original position.

```
Private Sub Form_DragDrop (source As Control, x As Single, Y As Single)
     Source.Move X, Y
End Sub
```

The **DragDrop** event positions the control with its top left corner at the
specified co-ordinates.

The DragIcon Property

When a control is dragged, a grey rectangle is used to represent it. The drag icon
that is displayed can be changed by using the **DragIcon** property. Particularly

useful if a picture is being dragged is to change the **DragIcon** property to the same icon as the picture that is being dragged. This has the effect of showing the picture itself moving as it is dragged.

```
Private Sub Form_Load ( )
     Picture1.DragIcon = Picture1.Picture
End Sub
```

The DragOver Event

The **DragIcon** property can be used in conjunction with the **DragOver** event to indicate that the control being dragged is in an area of the form that does not accept a drop. The usual way of doing this is to change the **DragIcon** property into an appropriate symbol, such as a stop sign, when it passes over the forbidden area – and back to normal when it leaves.

There is no code to prevent you from trying to drop the picture into this invalid area, but if you do so, nothing happens as there is no code in *Picture2*'s **DrapDrop** event processing.

```
Private Sub Picture2_DragOver (Source As Control), X As Single, Y As Single,
State As Integer)
If State = 0 Then
     Picture1.DragIcon = LoadPicture(C:\VB\ICONS\STOPICON.ICO)
If State = 1 Then
     Picture1.DragIcon = Picture1.Picture
End Sub
```

Keyboard Events

Visual Basic deals with keyboard events in a similar way to the button events associated with the mouse. In the main, keyboard events are:

- KeyPress.
- KeyDown.
- KeyUp.

The KeyPress Event

The **KeyPress** event (fig. 17.2) occurs whenever an ASCII key is pressed. The ASCII value of the key pressed is passed to the **KeyPress** event as an integer. In the example, the text in the text box is underlined if either the button is clicked or either "U" or "u" is pressed.

For example:

```
Private Sub Command1_Click ()
     If Text1.FontUnderline = true Then
```

```
            Text1.FontUnderline = false
            Else Text1.FontUnderline = true
        End If
End Sub

Private Sub Command1_KeyPress (KeyAscii As Integer)
If KeyAscii = Asc("U") Or KeyAscii = Asc("u") Then
    If Text1.FontUnderline = true Then
            Text1.FontUnderline = false
            Else Text1.FontUnderline = true
    End If
End If
End Sub
```

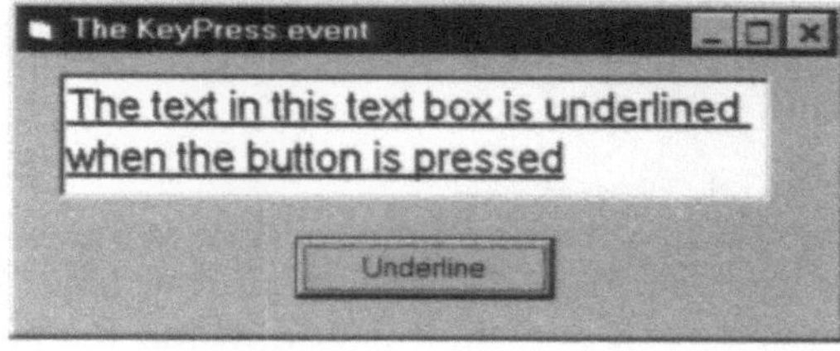

Fig. 17.2
The **KeyPress** event.

The KeyDown, KeyUp Events

The **KeyDown** and **KeyUp** events (fig. 17.3) occur when the user presses and releases a key while an object has the focus. **KeyUp** is always preceded by **KeyDown**.

```
Private Sub Picture1_KeyDown (keycode As Integer, Shift As Integer)

    ' if up arrow is pressed move to the previous list item
    If keycode = Key_Up Then MsgBox("Up arrow pressed")

    ' if down arrow is pressed move to the next list item
    If keycode = Key_Down Then MsgBox("Down arrow pressed")
End Sub
```

Fig. 17.3
Using up and down arrow.

While the **KeyPress** event can only be used to interpret ASCII characters, the **KeyDown** and **KeyUp** events can be used to interpret non-ASCII characters such as the navigation keys and the function keys.

18

Object Linking and Embedding (OLE)

Introduction

Object linking and embedding (OLE) allows programmers of Windows applications to create an application that can display information from other Windows applications and allows the user to edit that information within the application that created it. The Visual Basic OLE control is used to link and embed objects.

In this chapter you will learn about:

- Using the OLE control.
- Linking and embedding OLE objects.

Using OLE

An OLE object is a discrete data item that one application supplies to another, for example, a spreadsheet can supply a worksheet, or a range of cells. The class of the object gives the origination application, for example, MS Draw or PowerPoint (fig. 18.1).

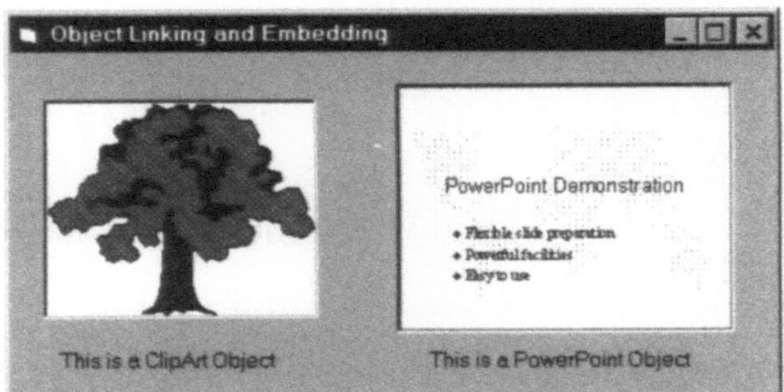

Fig. 18.1
Using OLE.

An application that can display other applications' objects is called a container application. In the Visual Basic application, the OLE object only exists in one OLE control and each OLE control can contain only one object at any particular time.

Linking and Embedding

OLE stands for object linking and embedding, but an object is either linked or embedded, not both. The **OLE** control is used to incorporate data into a Visual Basic application either by linking or embedding.

When an object is linked, the object's data can be accessed and modified by any application that has a link to it. The updated data is displayed in all the linked applications. The data is physically stored and maintained by the server application, not by the Visual Basic application.

When an object is embedded, a copy of the object's data is incorporated into the OLE control and is only available for that container application. The Visual Basic application has its own copy of the data, not the server application.

A document that comprises data objects from different Windows applications is called a compound document. Compound documents can, for example, consist of a Visual Basic defined form, containing a sheet from an Excel spreadsheet and a CorelDraw! picture.

The OLE Control

The OLE control (fig. 18.2) is used to link or embed objects into a Visual Basic application.

Fig. 18.2　*The OLE control.*

The **OLE** control is placed on the form in the same way as any other control: double click on the icon in the toolbox.

The **Insert Object** Dialog box is automatically displayed (fig. 18.3). This allows the user to specify the object type, that is, its class. If it is a new object (the default), the specified application is run and you can create the object.

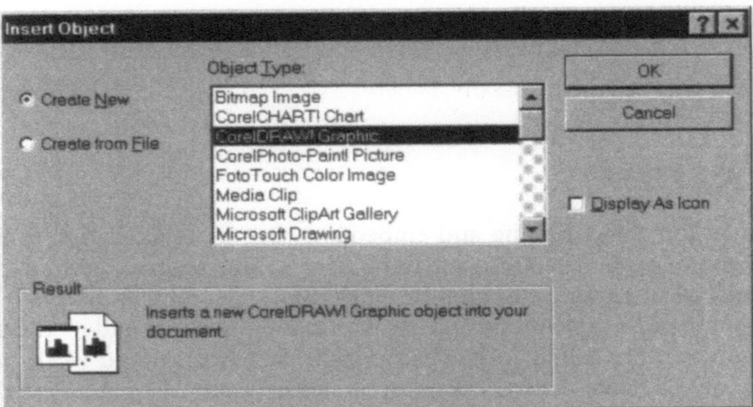

Fig. 18.3   *Inserting objects.*

If the object already exists, you select the **Create from File** option button and give
a file path (fig. 18.4).

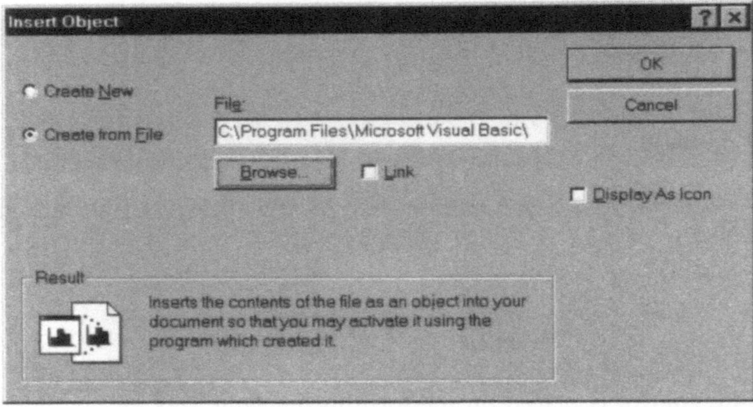

Fig. 18.4   *Creating new objects.*

You can restrict whether the OLE control can contain linked or embedded
controls by using the **OleTypeAllowed** property of the OLE control.

Value	Property
0	Linked (**vbOLELInked**)
1	Embedded (**vbOLEEmbedded**)
2	Either (**vbOLEEither**)
3	None (**vbOLENone**)

The OLE Pop-Up Menu

At design-time, if the user clicks the right mouse button on an OLE control, the following command list is displayed:

Command	Enabled in Menu when:
Insert Object	Opens the **Insert Object** dialog box so that the user can specify an object.
Paste Special	Creates an OLE object from the data in the clipboard.
Delete Embedded Object	Deletes an embedded OLE object.
Delete Linked Object	Deletes a linked OLE object.
Create Link	Creates an OLE link to an object that the user specifies.
Create Embedded Object	Embeds an OLE object that the user specifies.

Not all of these options may be displayed or be available, depending on the state of the application and the clipboard. For example, if the OLE control is empty, the **Delete** options are not displayed; if the clipboard is empty, the **Paste Special** option is not available.

If you find that you have inserted an incorrect object, you can delete the existing object and insert another linked or embedded object using these menu options. There is no need to delete an object before inserting a new one. Since the OLE control can only contain one object, the original object is deleted.

Using Paste Special

Objects can be inserted using the **Paste Special** option from the OLE pop-up menu. The **Paste Special** dialog is displayed, as shown in fig. 18.5.

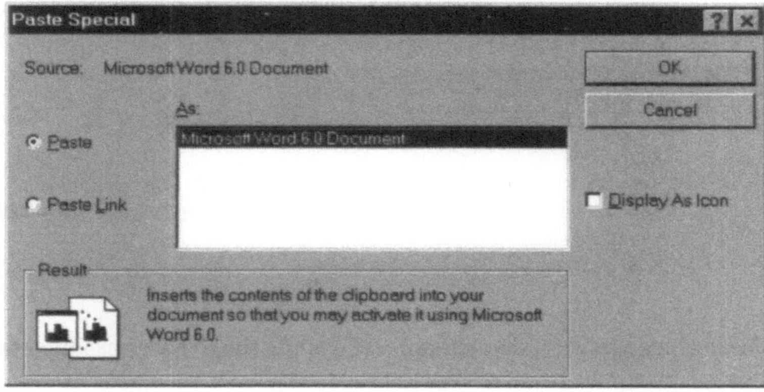

Fig. 18.5   *Using Paste Special.*

The **Paste Special** dialog displays the classes available for the object currently on the clipboard. You can choose whether the object is embedded (Paste) or linked (Paste Link). There is also a check box that allows you to display an icon instead of the object's image, which will speed up the screen refresh if the object takes a long time to display.

Creating OLE Objects at Run-Time

OLE control properties can be used at run-time to manipulate OLE objects. The most important properties that need setting in order to manipulate the objects are:

Property	Class
Class	Identifies the application that creates the object, for example, Excel.
OleTypeAllowed	Determines what type of objects are allowed: linked, embedded or both.
SourceDoc	Specifies the name of the file to become the OLE object.
SourceItem	Identifies the data item in the linked file.
Action	The action to be taken on a specific object.

For example (fig. 18.6):

```
Private Sub Form_Click ()
    Ole1.Class = "excelworksheet"              'Excel application
    Ole1.SourceDoc = "d:\excel\invest\invest.xls"   'file containing the data
    Ole1.SourceItem = "r37c2:r41c4"            'use rows 37 to 41, columns 2 to 4
    Ole1.Action = CreateLink                   'link to the object (not embed)
End Sub
```

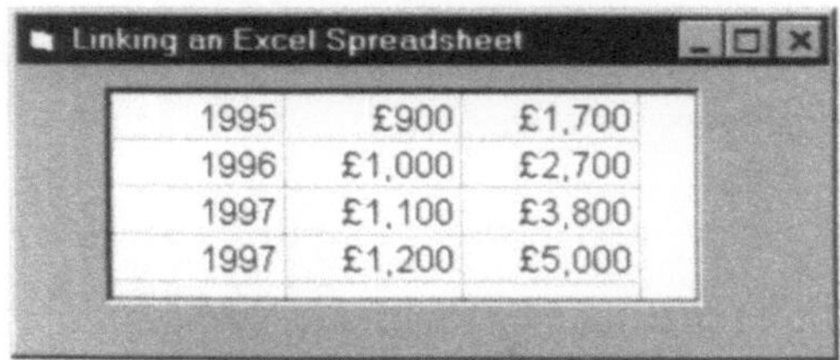

Fig. 18.6
Linking an Excel spreadsheet.

The **Action** property is not available at design-time. The possible settings for the **Action** property are:

Description	Value	Method
Creates an embedded object	0	**CreateEmbed**
Creates a linked object	1	**CreateLink**
Copies an object to the clipboard	4	**Copy**
Copies from the clipboard to an OLE container	5	**Paste**
Gets updated data from the embedded or linked application	6	**Update**
Opens an object	7	**DoVerb**
Closes an object and breaks the connection	9	**Close**
Deletes the object	10	**Delete**
Saves an object to a file	11	**SaveToFile**
Loads a saved object from a file	12	**ReadFromFile**
Displays the insert object dialog box	14	**InsertObjDlg**
Displays the paste special dialog box	15	**PasteSpecialDlg**
Updates the supported list of verbs	17	**FetchVerbs**
Saves an object in OLE file format	18	**SaveToOleFile**

Setting the **Action** property of an OLE control is similar in effect to invoking a method. The assignment of the **Action** property to a value causes an activity to take place before the next Visual Basic statement is executed, for example:

> *Ole1.Action = Copy*

This causes the contents of the OLE control to be copied onto the clipboard.

OLE Update Options Property

The **UpdateOptions** property of an OLE object determines when the OLE object in the OLE control is updated. It can have the following values:

Options	Meaning
vbOLEAutomatic	The OLE object is automatically updated whenever it is edited by the creating application. This is the default.
vbOLEFrozen	The OLE object is updated when the editing application saves its changes.
vbOLEManual	The OLE object is updated only when specifically requested to do so.

OLE AutoActivate Property

At run-time the user can activate an OLE object in an OLE control by using the **AutoActivate** property. The values of the **AutoActivate** property can be:

AutoActivate	Meaning
vbOLEActinateManual	This disables the facility. The object cannot be activated by the user at run time.
vbOLEActivateGetFocus	The object is activated whenever the OLE control gets the focus.
vbOLEActivateDoubleClick	The object is activated whenever the user double clicks the left mouse button on the OLE control at run-time. This is the default value.

OLE Verbs

The server application which supplies the data object defines a set of actions that may be carried out on that object. These actions are called verbs. Every object supports its own set of verbs. This can vary throughout the life of the application. For example, it may be possible to edit an object at some points and not at others.

The OLE control obtains the list of verbs from the server application and gives the user access to this list by accessing a set of OLE control properties. This allow the user to dynamically control the verbs that are supported at run-time. The properties are:

- **AutoVerbMenu.**
- **Verb.**
- **ObjectVerbs.**
- **ObjectVerbsCount.**

These are only available at run-time.

The AutoVerbMenu Property

At run-time, if the user points to an OLE object and clicks the right mouse button a pop-up menu appears if the **AutoVerbMenu** property is set to true, as shown in fig. 18.7. This is the default.
For example:

*Ole1.**AutoVerbMenu** = true*

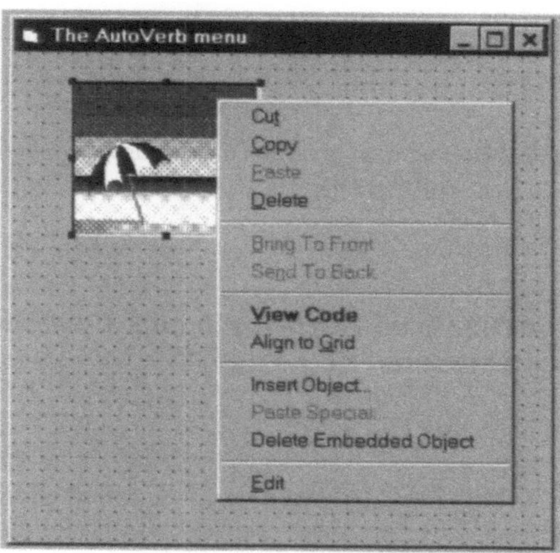

Fig. 18.7
AutoVerbMenu = true.

In this example of an embedded CorelDraw! object there are three verbs available, **Insert Object, Delete Embedded Object** and **Edit**.

The Verb Property

According to the current context and the server application, Visual Basic orders the available verbs sequentially, starting from 1.

Each OLE object has a default verb that is invoked when either the program or the user activates the OLE object. The program invokes the verb by setting the **Action** property to 7 (*OLE_ACTIVATE*). To set the verb for an OLE control you set the verb property to the index of a verb that is in the current verb list.

In addition, there are a set of standard verbs that are available for all OLE applications numbered from 0 to -3:

Value	Name	Meaning
0	**vbOLEPrimary**	Sets the **Verb** property to the default action for this OLE object in the current context.
-1	**vbOLEShow**	Activates the object for editing within the server application. If the object is able to be activated within its OLE control, then this takes place.
-2	**vbOLEOpen**	The object is opened with its server application in its own window.
-3	**vbOLEHide**	If the OLE object is embedded, the server application is hidden on the Windows screen.

The ObjectVerbsCount Properties

The **ObjectVerbsCount** property gives the number of verbs available at the current time.

The **ObjectVerbs** and **ObjectVerbsCount** properties allow the user to access the verbs supported by the application. For example:

MyOle.Verb = 2

This sets the verb to the second one in the current list for the *MyOle* object, and its server application in the current context.

The Updated Event

OLE controls support a special event called **Updated** which is called whenever the data in an OLE control is changed. The procedure declaration looks like this:

Private Sub OLE1_Updated (Code As Integer)

....

End Sub

The value of the **Code** parameter indicates how the object has changed. A set of standard values are defined:

Value	Constant	Meaning
0	**vbOLEChanged**	The object has changed.
1	**vbOLESaved**	The server application has saved the data in the OLE object.
2	**vbOLEClosed**	In the case of a linked object only, the server application has closed the file that the OLE control is linked to.
3	**vbOLERenamed**	In the case of a linked object only, the server application has renamed the file that the OLE control is linked to.

19

Using Files

Introduction

One of the most important features of Version 4 of Visual Basic is that it allows you to create and use database files, which greatly reduces the need for using other file systems. However, Visual Basic offers very good support for files outside database files. In this chapter you will learn about:

- Opening and closing files.
- Reading from files.
- Writing to files.

Supported File Types

Visual Basic supports two file types:

- ASCII files.
- Binary files.

It supports two sorts of access:

- Sequential.
- Random

In common with most programming languages, files need to be opened before they can be accessed.

Opening a File

Files are opened using the **Open** statement. They can be opened for:

- **Input** – the file can only be read.
- **Output** – the file can only be written to, from the start of the file.
- **Append** – the file can only be written to, from the end of the file.

For example:

> *Open "Project.doc" For Output As File #1*

- The file number can be any integer between 1 and 255.
- The "#" is optional.

The FreeFile Function

When opening a file, you need to specify a file number – errors can result if you use the same number twice. The **FreeFile** function can solve this problem, by returning the value of the next free file number.

> *TempFile = FreeFile( )*
> *Open "Text.tmp" For Input As File TempFile*

File Errors

If errors do occur when opening a file, Visual Basic provides excellent trapping mechanisms.

> *On Error Resume Next*
> *Open "Text.tmp" For Input As File 3*
> *If Err <> 0 Then*
> *   MsgBox("Error" + Str$(Err),48,"Error Handler")*
> *End If*

The **On Error Resume Next** statement before the **Open** statement instructs the program to continue at the line after the position where the error occurs. If an error occurs in the **Open** statement, it can be trapped by testing the error value which is returned as an integer in the variable **Err**. This can be converted for printout in a message box by using the **Str$** function.

Closing Files

When you have finished with a file, it is a good idea to close it – for two reasons. Firstly, so that you are not wasting memory and, secondly, so that if your program crashes there is less chance of data being lost.

> *Close #3*

- The "#" is optional.

If you forget to close a file, Visual Basic closes all your files before terminating.

Reading Files

To read an open file use the **Input$** function:

*Result = **Input$**(number of bytes, file identifier)*

For example:

*Information = **Input$** (512, #2)*

- The #2 specifies the file number; the "#" as always is optional.
- The 512 specifies the number of bytes that are to be read.

If you want to read the whole of the file, use the **LOF** function which returns the length of the file in bytes.
For example: ·

*SizeOfFile = **LOF** (3)*
*Information = **Input$** (SizeOfFile, #3)*

The maximum size of a string in Visual Basic is about 64K.

Reading ASCII Files

An ASCII text file is usually made up of lines – which the program is likely to want to read. Fortunately, Visual Basic provides a mechanism for reading lines of text.
Open the file for input, then use the **Line Input** statement.
For example:

Dim MyText As String
Line Input #3 As MyText

This reads one line of text into the string *MyText*. Visual Basic also has an end of file function which is set when the program reaches the end of the file:
For example:

Do Until EOF (3)
    Line Input #3 As MyText
    MsgBox (MyText)
Loop

This program reads successive lines from file #3 and output them to a message box.

Writing ASCII Files

To write to an ASCII file, open the file for **Output** or **Append** then use the **Print#** statement:

Print #1, "This is a line of text"

This prints the text to file #1.

- A CR/LF is automatically added to the end of the line of text.
- If you do not want to have a CR/LF added, add a semicolon to the end of the text.

Print #1 "This text ";
Print #1 "will all be printed on ";
Print #1 "one line"

Copying and Deleting Files

Visual Basic provides a simple way of copying an entire file – the entire contents of *First.txt* are copied to *Second.txt*:

FileCopy "First.txt", "Second.txt"

Files can be deleted with a single statement:

Kill "Temp.txt"

This is not simply a deletion that can be recovered later on – when you kill a file, it really is completely dead.

Random Access Files

Random access files can be read from and written to in any order. In order that they can behave like this, random access files must consist of equal sized records. Each record contains a collection of data about an object. The complete set of these records is called a file.

For example, a file of employee details may have records defined as:

```
Type Employee
    Name As String
    Address As String
    Age As Integer
    WorkNumber As Integer
    Salary As Double
End Type
```

Each record contains the details for one employee.

Using Random Access Files

The **Open** statement gives the file access type as **Random**. This opens a file called *Car.dbf* for random access. The file number is 3 and the length of each of the records is 78 bytes:

Open "Car.dbf" For Random As #3 Len=78

The **Get** statement is used to read from random access files. This example reads record 17 from file #3 into the variable *MyData*:

Get #3, 17, MyData

If you simply want to read the next record in the sequence you can omit the record number:

Get #3, , MyData

The **Put** statement is used to write to random access files. The example shown writes the contents of the variable *MyData* into record 23:

Put #2, 23, MyData

If you simply want to write to the next record in the sequence, you can omit the record number:

Put #2, , MyData

Binary Files

Binary files are really random access files with a record size of 1. They are read using **Get** and **Put** in the same way as random access files.

Open "Info.bin" For Binary As #3

The Seek Statement

You can move to a particular record in a binary file by using the **Seek** statement. You can then read sequentially through the file from that position.

Seek #1 67

This positions the file pointer to byte 67 so that the next sequential **Get** statement reads this byte.

Finding Files

Visual Basic provides three controls (fig. 19.1) for finding files:

- The **DriveListBox** control.
- The **DirListBox** control.
- The **FileListBox** control.

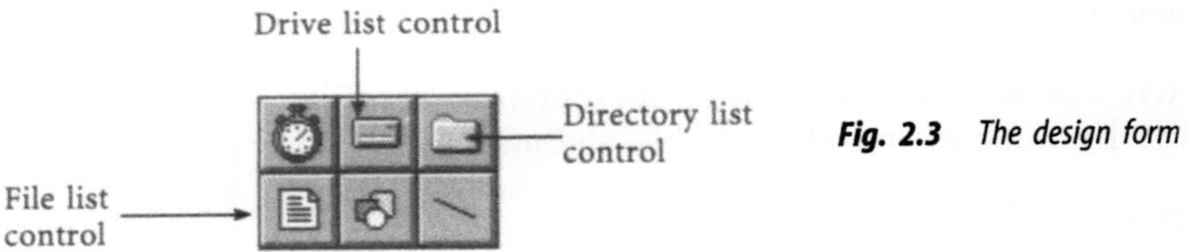

Fig. 2.3   *The design form*

These three controls can be used co-operating together to provide the familiar interface for browsing through you disks and finding the file you want, as shown in fig. 19.2.

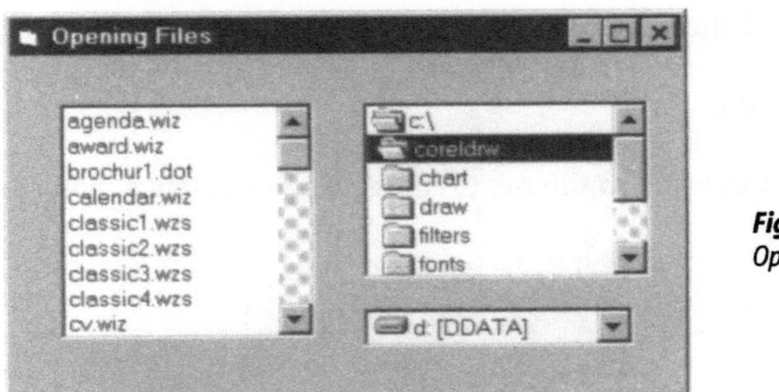

Fig. 19.2
Opening files

The FileListBox

The **FileListBox** control has similar properties to an ordinary list box, however there are several special properties.

The **Path** property specifies the current directory for the **FileListBox**. This can be set at run-time:

*File1.**Path** = "D:\VISUALB\ICONS"*

The **Pattern** property specifies which files should be displayed:

*File.**Pattern** = "*.ICO"*

The FileName Property

The **FileName** property contains the name of the file that is currently selected:

*file1.**FileName** = "D:\VISUALB\PROG.TXT"*

If changing the **FileName** property alters the path, a **PathChange** event and also a **PatternChange** event occur.

Linking the Controls

In order for the three controls to be synchronised so that they work together, a small amount of code is required. Double click on the drive control; this takes you into the template subroutine for processing the change event. Add the line of code as shown.

```
Private Sub Drive1_Change ( )
    Dir1.Path = Drive1.Drive
End Sub
```

The added line sets the path for the directory control to the new drive selected. Similarly, modifying the code for the directory change event sets the path for the file list control to the new path selected.

```
Private Sub Dir1_Change ( )
    File1.Path = Dir1.Path
End Sub
```

20
Databases

Introduction

Visual Basic 4 allows you edit and update data from a wide range of databases, including Access, FoxPro, Paradox and dBase.

The data control uses the Microsoft Jet database engine, the same engine used in Access which gives great flexibility in accessing standard database formats and creating applications that access databases. In this chapter you will learn about:

- Creating databases.
- Creating and using tables and attributes.
- Updating databases.

Using Databases

- Visual Basic contains the Access database engine in the form of a dynamic link library.
- Access offers facilities such as field validation and data integrity checking.
- Visual Basic has far more facilities for designing forms and screen objects than Access.
- Third parties are providing a growing range of accessories and controls which extend the capabilities of Visual Basic.

Some applications run faster if written in Visual Basic and the code size is likely to be less than if written in Access. However, Access provides a range of database manipulation facilities which needs to be coded if you use Visual Basic. Using Access to create the database and Visual Basic for the user interface is a useful approach that many application designers use.

Database Jargon

In relational databases, data is organised into tables, as shown in fig. 20.1 for example.

Title	Forename	Surname	Dept.	Ext. no.
Mr.	Edward	Codd	HL2	4502
Ms.	Hilary	Taylor	PT2	6702

Fig. 20.1 *Database tables.*

- Each row in the table represents the data on a single object. Rows are sometimes called records.
- Each column in a table is a specific sort of information, for example, the *Department* name.
- Each of the entries in the table, given by the intersection of a row and column, is a field.
- In order to find the information you want, for example, all the people in department HL2, you need to construct a query.
- If you are performing queries based on a particular column, you can construct an index based on that column which greatly speeds up your searches.

Creating a Database

To illustrate how Visual Basic creates an Access database, this chapter follows the creation of a simple database that has only one table containing traffic signs, with a name and description.

In order to create an Access table:

- Select the **Data Manager** option from the **Add-Ins** menu.
- Open the **File** menu and choose the **New Database** option.

A screen similar to the one shown in fig. 20.2 appears.

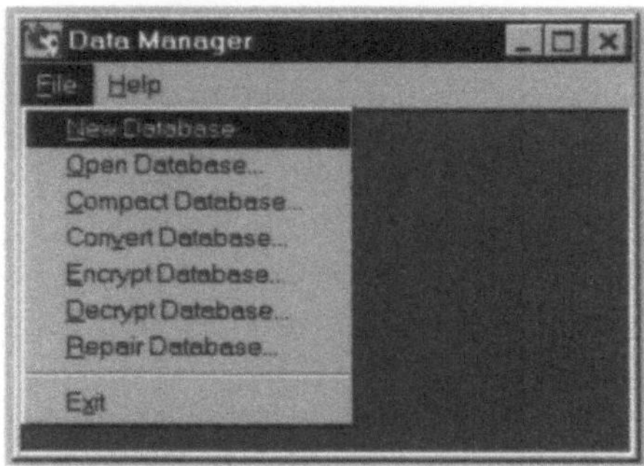

Fig. 20.2
Creating a new database.

The screen shown in fig. 20.3 is displayed.
Select the **New Database** option.

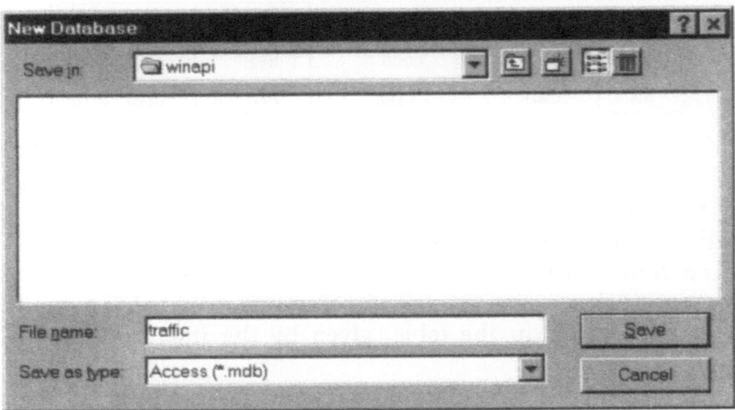

Fig. 20.3   *Naming the new database.*

- Specify the file name of the database and click **Save**.
- The database has been created. The window shown in fig. 20.4 is displayed. The next stage is to create the tables that it contains. Click on the **New** button.

Fig. 20.4   *Creating new tables.*

- In fig. 20.4 the name of the database *TRAFFIC.MDB* is shown at the top of the form.

Specifying Fields

The database and the single table it contains have now been named. The next stage is to specify the fields that make up this table.

- After clicking on **New** the screen shown in fig. 20.5 appears.

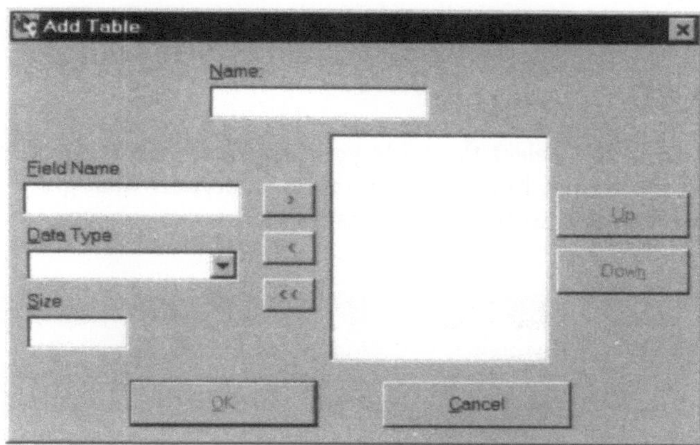

Fig. 20.5   *Adding a table to the database.*

First enter the name of the table, *traffic*.
There are three fields to be entered in this table:

- The name of the traffic sign
- A description of the traffic sign
- The traffic sign icon.

To add the name field:

- Click on the *Field name* field.
- Insert the field name *Name* as type **Text** and a size of 20 characters.
- Click on the right-pointing button which moves the entry to the right-side text box.
- Repeat the process, adding another two fields: *Description* – type **Text** – 40 characters long, and *Icon*, type **Long Binary** as shown in fig. 20.6.

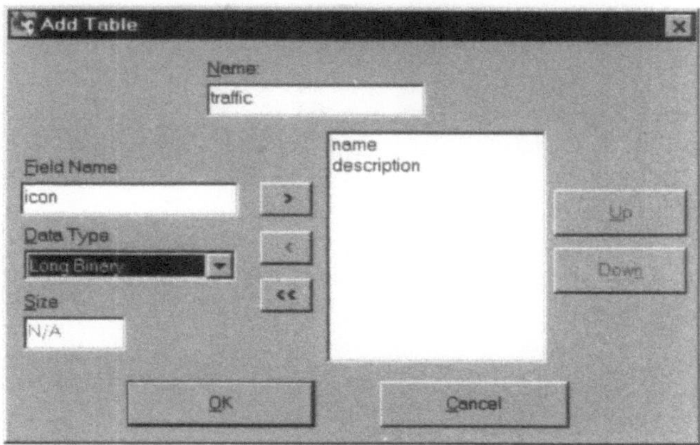

Fig. 20.6

- Click on OK to return to the Data Manager.

Adding an Index

- To add an index, select the table you have just created by clicking on it.
- Click on the design button in the tables/querydefs dialog.
- The screen shown in fig. 20.7 is displayed.

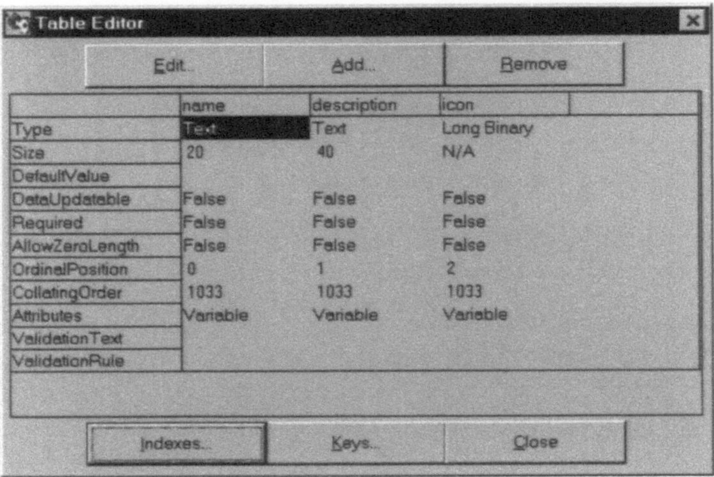

Fig. 20.7

- Click on the **Indexes** button in the table editor dialog.
- The screen shown in fig. 20.8 appears.

Fig. 20.8
Adding an index (1).

- Click on the **Add** button.
- The screen shown in fig. 20.9 is displayed.

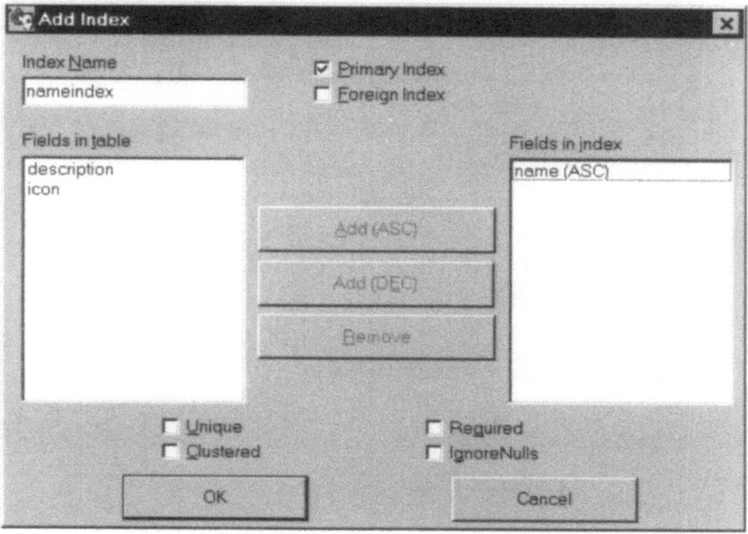

Fig. 20.9 *Adding an index (2).*

- Click on the field in the *Fields in table* list to select the *name* field as the index.
- Click on the add (ASC) field to make this an index.
- Click on the *Primary Index* check box to make this a primary index, where duplicates are not allowed.
- Click on OK to return to the data manager.

Adding Data

- Select the table that you want to add to by clicking on its name in the tables/querydefs dialog.
- The traffic table is displayed as shown in fig. 20.10.
- Click on **Add**.
- Enter the *Name, Description* and *Icon* as prompted.
- When the record has been added, click on the **Update** button.
- Repeat the process to add more records.
- Click on **Close** to return to the data manager.

A database has been defined which contains one table. Records have been entered into this table. The next stage is to develop an application that will allow this data to be read, changed and added to.

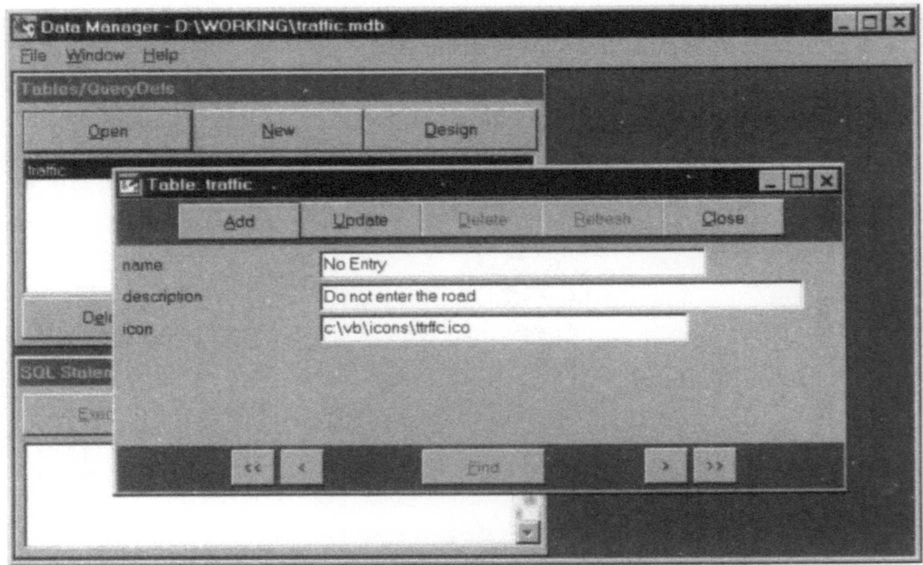

Fig. 20.10   *Adding data to the traffic table.*

The Data Control

The **Data** control (fig. 20.11) connects your Visual Basic application to the database and opens a specified database table or a set of records based on an SQL query on the database.

- After the data control has been connected to the database, you can bind data-aware controls to the data control.
- The data control is used to choose the record that you want to view. The data-aware controls that the data control is connected to are used to display the fields of that record.

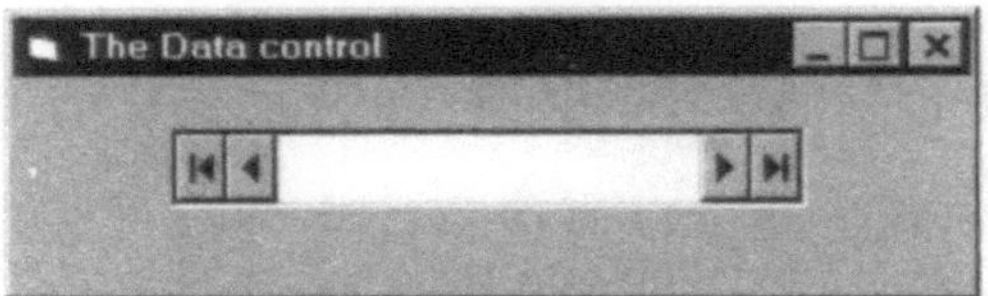

Fig. 20.11   *The **Data** control.*

- If the user clicks on the leftmost arrow, the first record is displayed.
- The other left-pointing arrow moves to the previous record.
- Similarly, the two right arrows move to the last record and the next record in the file.

Connecting the Data Control

- In order to connect the data control to the database, you need to set the **DataBaseName** property to the name of the database *TRAFFIC.MDB*.
- The **RecordSource** property of the data control accesses the database and determines what tables exist in the specified database.
- Since there is only one table in this database, this appears in the Settings box.
- If there are multiple tables, you can select one by clicking the down arrow next to the box and making your choice.

Viewing the Database

In order to view this database, a form similar to the one shown in fig. 20.12 can be created.

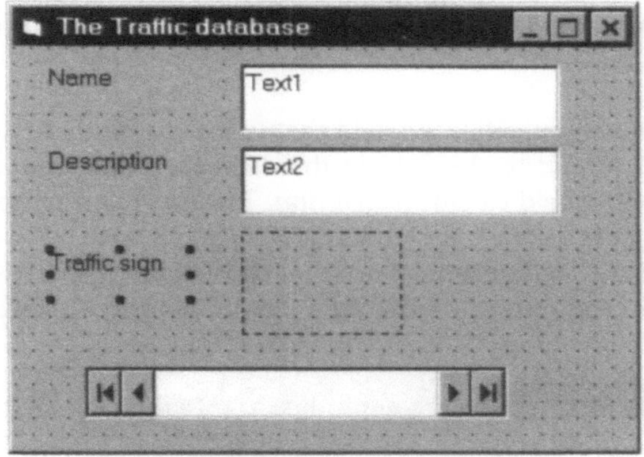

Fig. 20.12
The traffic database – design screen.

- Set the **MultiLine** property of the text box to true.
- The traffic sign is displayed in an image box. Set the **Stretch** property of the image box to true.

Bound Properties

The final stage is to bind the individual controls to fields in the database. Visual Basic allows you to bind a several controls:

- Text boxes.
- Images boxes.
- Picture boxes.
- Check boxes.
- Labels.

In addition there are three special controls which are data-aware variants of other controls available as custom controls. These controls are:

- **DBGrid.**
- **DBCombo.**
- **DBList.**

Properties for Data-Aware Controls

There are three new properties for the five "data-aware" controls:

- The **DataSource** property.
- The **DataField** property.
- The **DataChanged** property.

The **Data Source** property specifies:

- The data control to which you are binding. In this example there is only one data control, called *Data1*.

The **DataField** (fig. 20.13) property specifies the field that you are binding to. In this example the top text box is bound to the field in the database called *Name*. The second text box is bound to the field called *Description*. The final picture box is bound to the *Icon* field.

You can type the name of the **DataSource** and the **DataField** properties; however, Visual Basic offers you the option of selecting from a drop-down list.

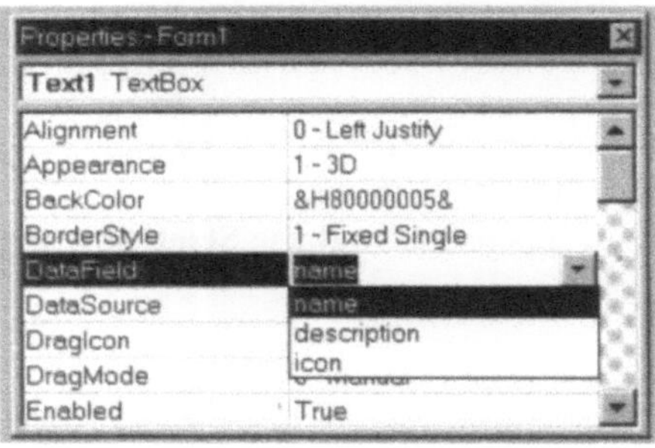

Fig. 20.13
*Setting the **DataField** property.*

The DataChanged Property

- If a record is modified, the **DataChanged** property is set to true.
- This control is only available at run-time.
- Visual Basic automatically updates the database only if this is set to true.

The Traffic Sign Program

The traffic sign program is now completed; however, no descriptions have yet been added. This can be done by running the program and typing the description in the text box, as shown in fig. 20.14.

The records can be stepped through by using the data control as shown in fig. 20.14.

Fig. 20.14
The traffic database.

Duplicating the Data Control

The Data control allows you to move through your records and to amend them. If you want to duplicate the functionality of the data control, you can do this by setting the **Visible** property to false and attaching some code to another control. The methods that you need are:

- MoveNext.
- MoveFirst.
- MoveLast.
- MovePrevious.

Adding and Deleting Records

If you want to add or delete records (fig. 20.15), you need to create a new control and to attach some code to it.

- The **AddNew** method clears all the fields in a record in preparation for a new record to be added.
- After using **AddNew**, the **Update** method is automatically invoked to save the data to the database.

Fig. 20.15
Adding records to the database.

The updating is dealt with after clicking on the *Add a Record* button. The code associated with this event is:

```
Private Sub Command1_Click ( )
        Data1.Recordset.AddNew
        Text1.SetFocus
End Sub
```

- *Data1* is the name of the data control.
- The **RecordSet** is the current set of records.
- The **SetFocus** method ensures that the cursor is placed on the *Text1* box. *Text1* is said to "have the focus".

Deleting a Record

The current record can be deleted by using the **Delete** method.

- Create a command button called *"Delete a record"* and add the following code to its click event:

```
Data1.Recordset.Delete
```

After deleting the current record, move either to the next or to the first record if the end of the file has been reached:

```
Data1.RecordSet.MoveNext
If Data1.Recordset.EOF Then Data1.Recordset.MoveFirst
```

- The **EOF** property refers to the end of file. If the last record has been deleted, the first record is displayed.
- The property **BOF** refers to the beginning of file.

If only the above line is used, the current record is deleted from the database but remains displayed on the screen. Therefore it is a good idea to shift the focus to the next record by using the **MoveNext** method to display the next record.

Adding a New Field to a Table

Most databases consist of more than one table. In a relational database, tables are joined by having one column in common.

To add a further field to the database, select the **Data Manager** from the **Add-Ins** menu option.

- Select **Open Database** from the **File** menu.
- Select the table required and then choose **Design** on the **Tables/QueryDefs** menu.
- Select **Add** from the **Fields** table and insert the new field as prompted in fig. 20.16

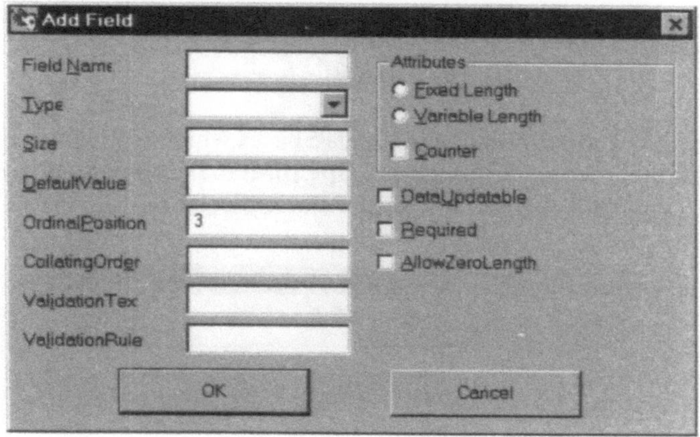

Fig. 20.16 *Adding a new field.*

Adding a New Table

- Click on the add button on the table/querydefs dialog.
- Add the details of the new table in the tables dialog.

The Data Form Designer

A new feature of Version 4 of Visual Basic is the data form designer, which produces a form for reading, and amending data in a database. To run it, click on the **Data Forms Designer** option on the **Add-Ins** menu. The design screen as shown in fig. 20.17 is displayed.

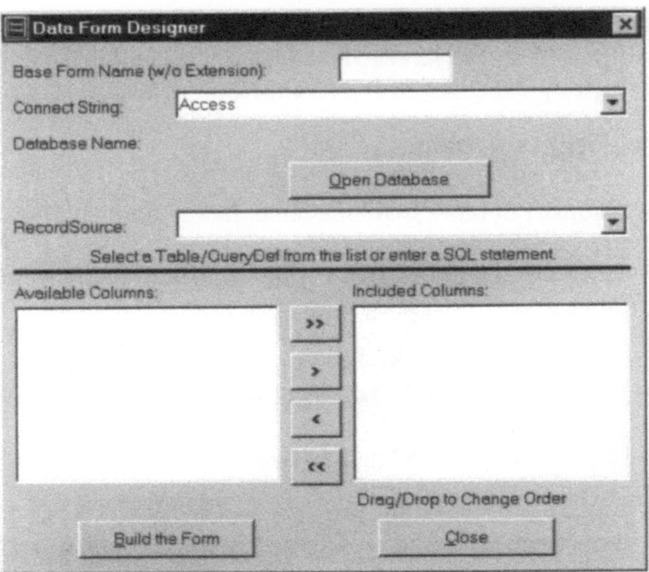

Fig. 20.17   *The data form designer.*

Visual Basic has a number of sample databases which can be used to show how the forms designer works. Click on the **Open Database** button and choose the file called *Biblio* (fig. 20.18) from the Visual Basic directory.

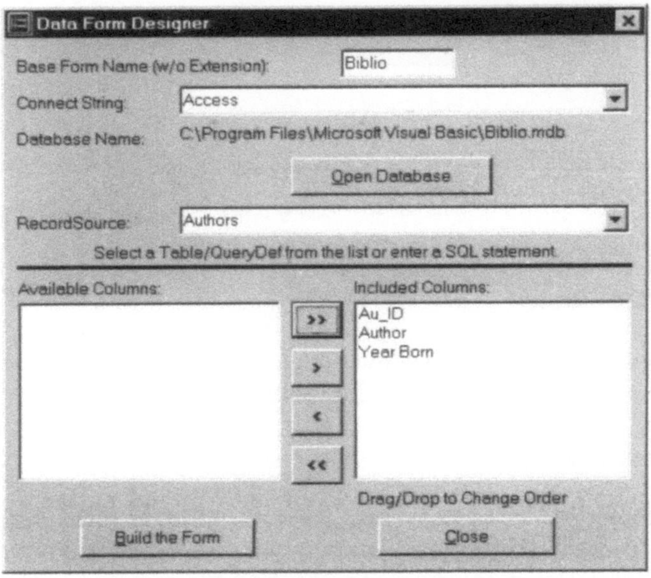

Fig. 20.18   *The biblio database.*

- Click on the button with the two right facing arrows to move all the fields to the right list – these fields will be available when the application is run.
- Specify the form name at the top of the form.
- Click on the **Build the Form** button.
- Click on the **Close** button.
- Change the name of the startup form to the name of the form you have just created with the data forms designer in the **Projects** page of the **Options** option on the **Tools** menu.
- Run the application.

The running application is shown in fig. 20.19.

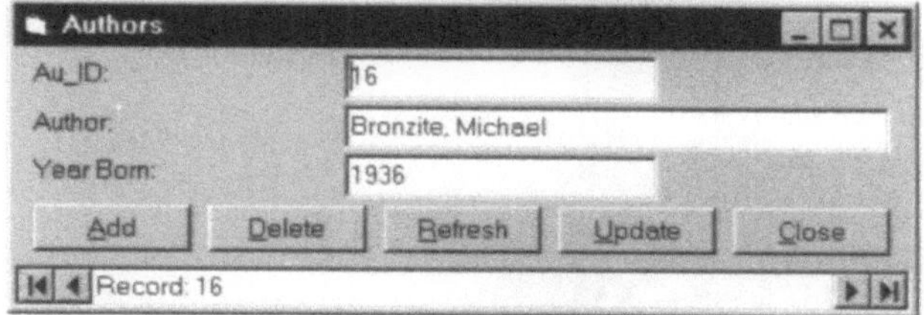

Fig. 20.19   *The running database application.*

All of the buttons are functional and you can browse through the database using the data control.

21
Examples

Creating a Simple Project

This section supports Chapters 1, 2 and 3.

The purpose of this session is to create a project with one form. When you click on a button, the current time and date will be displayed.

- Start Visual Basic.
- Create a new project.
- Add a text box to your form.
- Add a command button to your form.
- Try moving the command button and the text box by selecting and dragging.
- Try re-scaling the button and boxes.
- When you select the button, the properties window changes to show the button properties.
- Change the **Caption** property of the button to *Press me.*
- Change the properties of the text box so that it does not display the text *Text1.*
- The function that displays the current date and time is called **Now**. To find out how to use it select **Help** and use the **Search** facility to find **Now**.

When the button is pressed you want the text box to display the text "The current date and time are" followed by the date and time. The code associated with the button press event can be reached by double clicking on the button.

- Double click on the button and put in a line of code to display the required message.
- Run the program.
- What happens when you press tab?

When the program is running satisfactorily, create an EXE file and install it in a Window's group so that it can be invoked by clicking on an icon.

Creating a Large Form

The purpose of this session is to create a substantial form, which uses a wide range of features including combo boxes, lists, option buttons and check boxes. The aim of the form is to collect data from car buyers. Your completed form should be similar to the one shown in fig. 21.1.

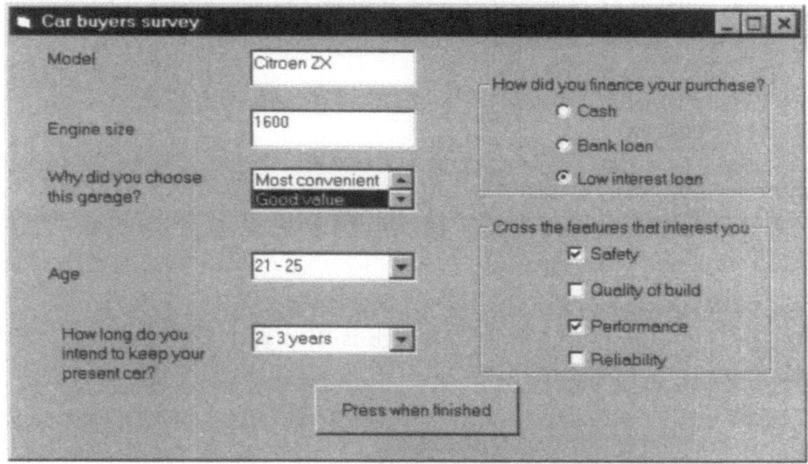

Fig. 21.1 *The car buyers' survey.*

- Create a new project.
- The option buttons and the check boxes need to be grouped together in a frame. The frame must be drawn first.
- The control where the user states his age is a drop-down combo.
- The control where the purchaser states why he chose that garage is a type of combo box called a drop-down list.
- The control where the purchaser states his age is a list.

Controlling Control Properties

The aim of this session is to control a few of the properties of a text box.

- Create a new project.
- Create a form similar to the one shown in fig. 21.2.

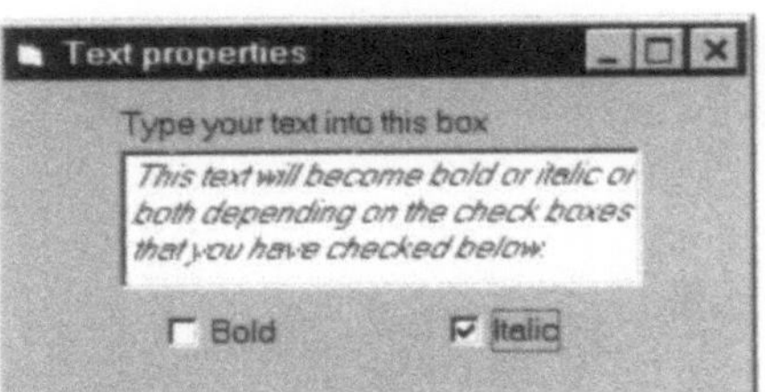

Fig. 21.2
Using text box properties.

- Set the **MultiLine** property of the text box to true.
- Go to the **Click** event for the *Bold* check box (double click on the check box) and write the code for changing the **Text** property to bold if the check box is set (has a value of 1) and changing it back to non-bold if it is cleared again.
- Carry out a similar action for the italic check box.

File Delete Program

This exercise supports Chapter 7.

The aim of this session is to provide the user interface for a program that will delete a file.

- Create a new project.
- When the program is run, a message is displayed giving the user information about this program (fig. 21.3).

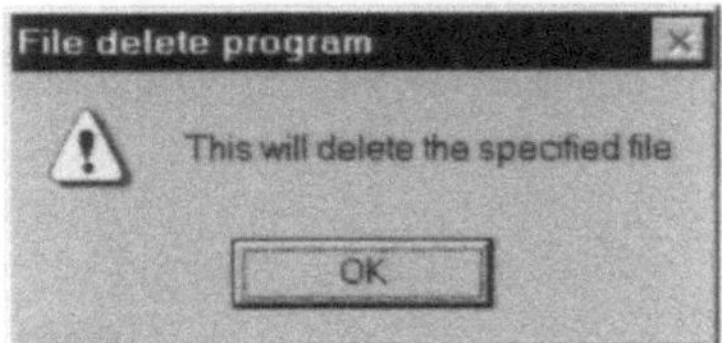

Fig. 21.3
Using message boxes.

- The user is then prompted for the name of the file (fig. 21.4).

Fig. 21.4   Using **InputBox**.

- On selecting the file name, the message box shown in fig. 21.5 is displayed.

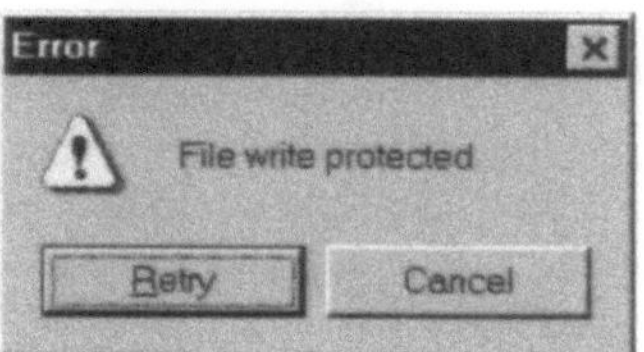

Fig. 21.5
The error dialog box.

- If *Cancel* is selected, the program is stopped by using the **END** statement.
- If *Retry* is selected, the user is prompted to supply another file name using the previous message box.

Finance Company

These exercises support Chapters 8, 9, 10 and 11.

A finance company needs a program to determine whether or not a client should be given a bank loan. The rules that they use are as follows:

Monthly income	Minimum loan	Maximum loan
Less than 500	–	0
500–700	500	(income – outgoings * 2) + 500
701–1000	500	(income – outgoings * 2.5) + 500
1001–1500	1000	(income – outgoings * 2.8) + 1000
greater than 1500	1000	income – outgoings * 3.0) + 2000

The maximum loan is reduced by £500 for each dependent child.

- Create a new project.
- Create a new form that allows the user to specify the following:
- Monthly income.
- Monthly outgoings on servicing existing bank loans.
- Monthly outgoings on servicing credit debts.
- Monthly outgoings on mortgage.
- Monthly outgoings on other loans.
- Size of loan requested.
- Number of dependent children.

The total outgoings is the sum of the monthly outgoings.

The loan is approved if the amount requested is greater than the minimum and less than the maximum. When the user has specified all this information, the program must indicate if the loan is approved or not.

Zoo Database

In a zoo, the animals have a different diet depending on their type. The object of this session is to produce a program that will request the name of the animal and will specify the type of food the animal needs.

The following animals eat the following foods:

Type of animal	Type of food	Type of animal	Type of food
lion	meat	chimpanzee	bananas
zebra	grass	seal	fish

The zoo has the following animals:

Name	Type of animal	Name	Type of animal
Clarence	lion	Sally	zebra
Henry	lion	Zoe	zebra
Bertha	lion	Martin	zebra
Barbara	chimpanzee	Simon	seal
Bill	chimpanzee	Winnie	seal

The information above will need to be stored in two two-dimensional arrays:

- The user selects the name of the animal from a combo list.
- The type of foods that the animal wants is displayed.

Changing Text Styles

This exercise supports Chapter 12.

This program uses menus and some additional properties of text boxes.

When the program is run, it displays the form shown in fig. 21.6.

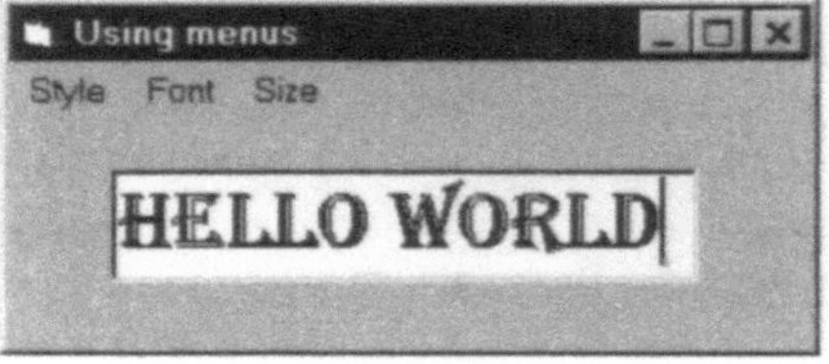

Fig. 21.6
Using menus.

When the user selects the *Style* option, he can choose between "**Bold**" and "*Italic*". If the text is not bold it is made bold, and vice versa.

When the user selects the *Font* option, he can choose between the following fonts: "`Courier New`", "**Arial**" and "Times New Roman".

When the user selects *Size*, he can choose between 10, 20 or 30 point text.

Whatever action the user selects is reflected in changes to the "Hello world" text which is displayed in the text box.

- The **FontBold** property of text boxes is either true or false.
- The **FontItalic** property of text boxes is either true or false.

- The **FontSize** property controls the size.
- The **FontName** property controls the font used.

MDI Viewer

This exercise supports Chapter 13.

The aim of this application is to allow the user to specify up to four child windows and to display a different BMP file within each one.

- Create a new project.
- Create an MDI form and four child windows

Note after you have selected the option **New MDI Form** from the **File** menu that this option is light grey in colour – indicating that it cannot be used. Visual Basic only allows one MDI form per application.

Ensure that the first form to be displayed on running the program is the MDI form.

At run-time, assign a BMP file to each of the four child windows using the **LoadPicture** function.

Create a menu for the MDI form which has the following options:

- Tile.
- Cascade.
- Minimise all child forms.
- Maximise all child forms.

Forms can be minimised by using the **WindowState** property, for example:

Form1.WindowState = 0

Assigning this property to 0 (the default) is normal display, 1 is minimised, 2 is maximised.

The form, after selecting the cascade option (the default), will look like that shown in fig. 21.7:

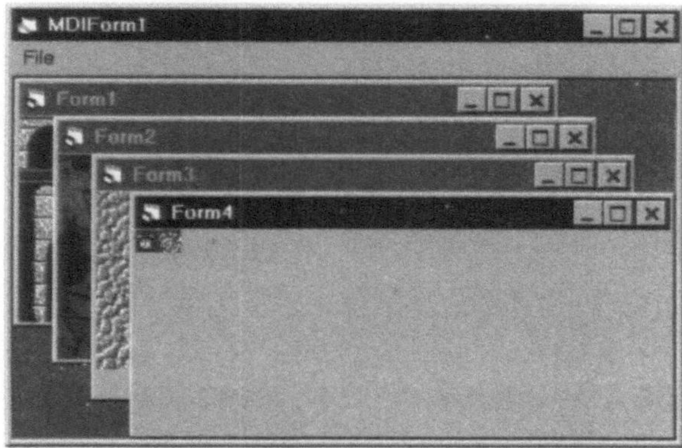

Fig. 21.7
Cascaded child forms.

After selecting the *Tile* option, the form will look like the one shown in fig. 21.8.

Fig. 21.8
Tiling forms.

After selecting the minimise option the following minimised forms are displayed:

Fig. 21.9   Minimised forms.

Any of the forms can be displayed by double clicking on them in the usual way.

Creating and Using Grids

This exercise supports Chapter 14.

The aim of this program is to create a grid that contains name and address details.

Start a new project. Create a grid – the size of the grid does not matter. Your form will look similar to the one shown in fig. 21.10.

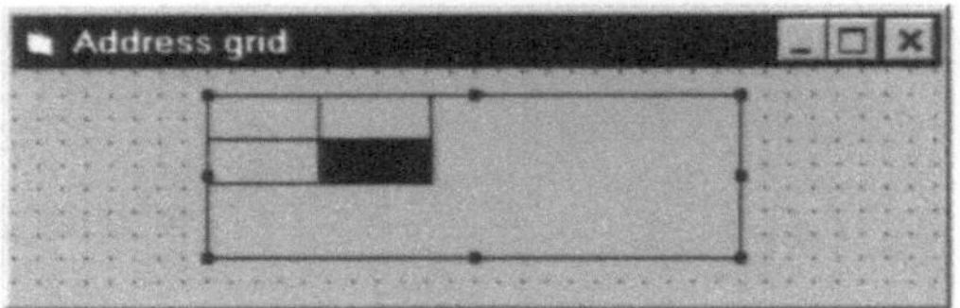

Fig. 21.10
The initial address grid.

When your program runs, it will look like the one shown in fig. 21.11.

Fig. 21.11
The completed address grid.

The text in grids cannot be added at design-time. You will need to put code in the **Form_Load** subroutine to enter the data.

The widths of the columns will need to be adjusted – you can do this by using the *ColWidth(column_number)* property of columns.

The top row and the leftmost column are fixed. You cannot write text to fixed cells, but you can alter which cells are fixed at run-time. Therefore, in order to write to fixed cells, you need to make sure the cells are not fixed, write to them and then make them fixed.

Deleting Grid Rows

The aim of this session is to amend the previous program so that you can delete a row.

Your form will look like that shown in fig. 21.12 when the program is running.

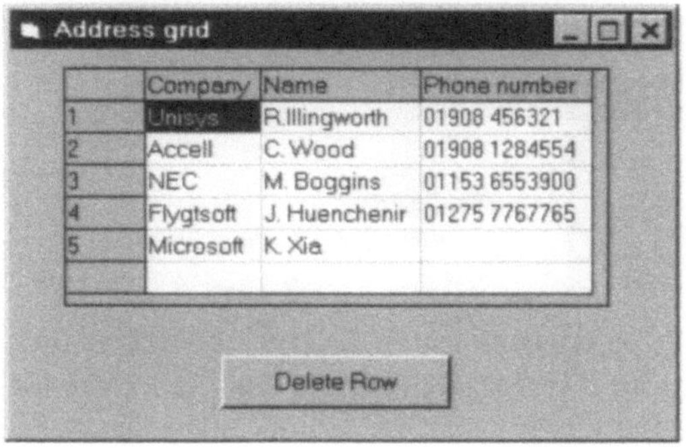

Fig. 21.12
Deleting rows.

The only addition is that a button has been added.

When the button is pressed, the row that the current cell is in is selected, and the message box shown in fig. 21.13 is displayed.

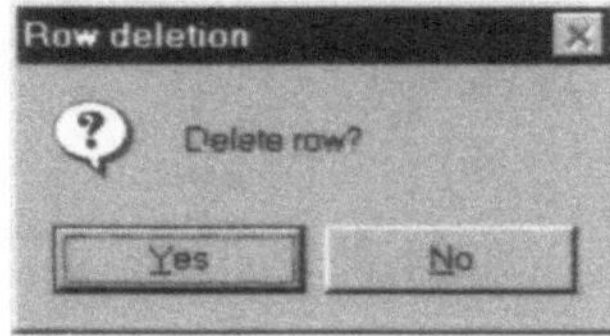

Fig. 21.13
The delete row message box.

If you select OK, the row is deleted using the **RemoveItem** method.

Importing Graphics

This exercise supports Chapter 15.
The aim of this program is to create an icon viewer.

- Start a new project.
- Create a image box that contains a graphic.
- Create a text box and a caption that will prompt the user for a file name.

If the user specifies an existing icon file, the image is displayed. If the file does not exist, a dialog box should display an error message.
The form will look similar to the one shown in fig. 21.14 if the icon is found.

Fig. 21.14
The icon viewer.

If the icon is not found, it displays a dialog box similar to the one shown in fig. 21.15.

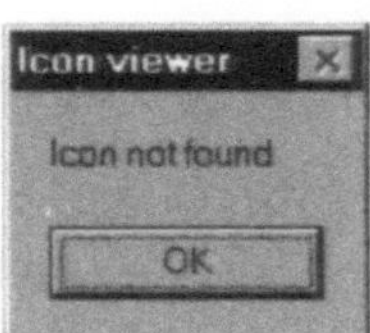

Fig. 21.15
The icon not found message box.

This icon is rather small, but you can make it larger by increasing the size of the image box and using the **Stretch** property. You can do this either by amending this property of the picture box control at design time or at run-time. It will give a display similar to the one shown in fig. 21.16.

Fig. 21.16
Using the Stretch property to increase the image size.

Drawing Pi Charts

There are four categories of people for the purposes of unemployment statistics. The purpose of the program is to prompt the user to supply the percentage figures of:

- Full-time employed
- Part-time employed
- Unemployed
- Education.

Create a form that prompts the user to supply the percentage figures for each of these categories and then displays the results in a similar form to that shown in fig. 21.17.

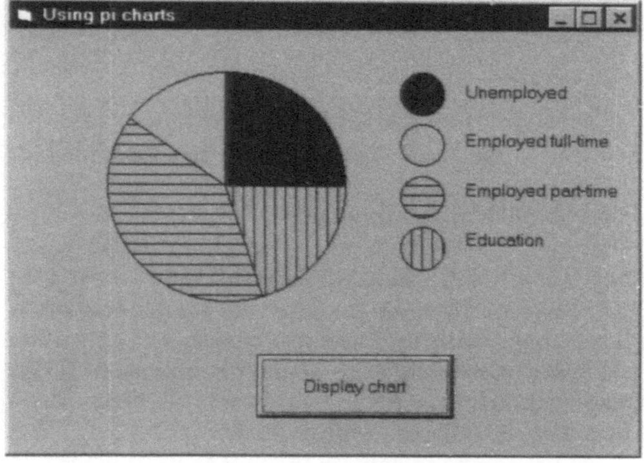

Fig. 21.17   *Using pi charts.*

The **Circle** method should be used to draw the pie-shaped sections – remembering to put a minus sign before the start and end positions of the section. To fill the sections, set the **FillStyle** property of the form to a different value before using the **Circle** method to draw each section.

A common mistake when drawing pi charts is that when a parameter is missed, such as the **color** parameter in this application (**color** is the fourth parameter), you must have a pair of commas as shown below. If you omit the second comma of the pair, you will get an unexpected result.

*Circle (2000, 1500), 1100, , – 0.0001 * pi, – 0.5 * pi*

On your input form, you should check that the total of the figures adds up to 100%.

Printing to a Picture Box

These exercises support Chapter 16.

Create a form like the one shown in fig. 21.18. The purpose of the exercise is to print a sample of text into a picture box.

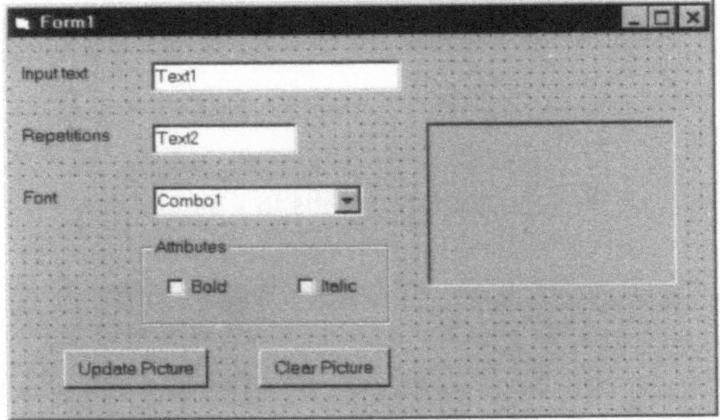

Fig. 21.18   *The application design screen.*

This form has the following components:

- A label box, *Label1*, with the caption *Input Text*.
- A text box, *Text1*, for the user to enter the sample text.
- A label box, *Label2*, with the caption *Repetitions*.
- A text box, *Text2*, for the user to enter the number of times *Text1* is to be printed into *Picture1*.
- A label box, *Label3*, with the caption *Font*.
- A drop-down list combo to contain the font to be used when *Text1* is printed into *Picture1*. The fonts available in the system can be obtained from the arrays **Screen.Fonts** and **Printer.Fonts** at run-time. If you allow the user to specify an invalid screen font, then a run-time error will occur.
- A frame with the caption *Attributes*.
- A check box, *Check1*, in the *Attributes* frame with the caption *Bold*.
- A check box, *Check2*, in the *Attributes* frame with the caption *Italic*.
- A command button with the caption *Update Picture*. When this button is clicked, the text in *Text1* will be printed in *Picture1* with the appropriate number of repetitions. The text will use the selected screen font and be bold and italic as appropriate.
- A command button with the caption *Clear Picture*. When this button is pressed, the text in *Picture1* will be cleared.
- A picture box, *Picture1*, into which the text is to be printed. The user should not be able to select this control.

At run-time the list of fonts must be assembled and one of them chosen as the current font. The initial value of repetitions should be one. Ensure that the non-numeric content of *Repetitions* does not cause an error.

The value of the font and attributes to be used can be set either when they are selected or when *Update Picture* is clicked.

Printing Tabular Data

Change the window from the previous example so that each repetition starts at the next tab position.

Allow the user to set the column width by adding some extra controls to the form:

- Add a horizontal scroll bar, *Hscroll1*, that ranges from 4 to 20. This will be used to vary the width of the columns in *Picture1*. Set the value of **Small-Change = 1** and **Large-Change = 4**.
- Add a label box, *Label4*, with the caption *Tab width*.
- Add a label box, *Label5*, that will hold the current value of the horizontal scroll bar. Make the data right-aligned.

The form should now look like the one shown in fig. 21.19.

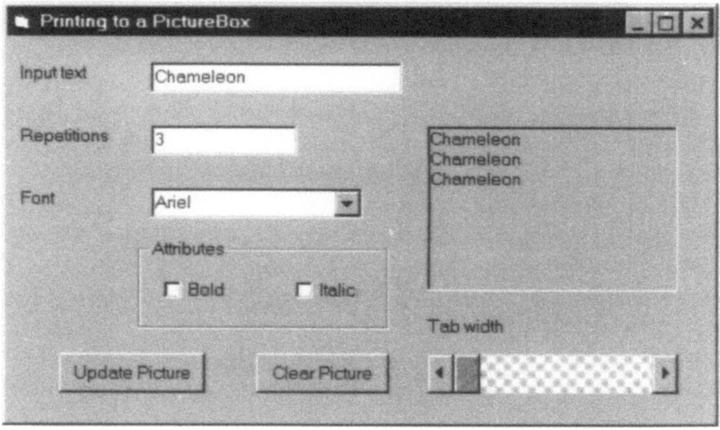

Fig. 21.19　*Printing to a PictureBox.*

Ensure that the column width is set to the minimum width at the start, and that the current column width is displayed as it is changed. Check that the user specified tab width is used when *Update Picture* prints to the picture box.

Printing at a Specific Location Using Format

This session uses the **Format** functions to print information in a chosen pattern. It also makes use of the facilities to print at a particular location within the chosen area (fig. 21.20).

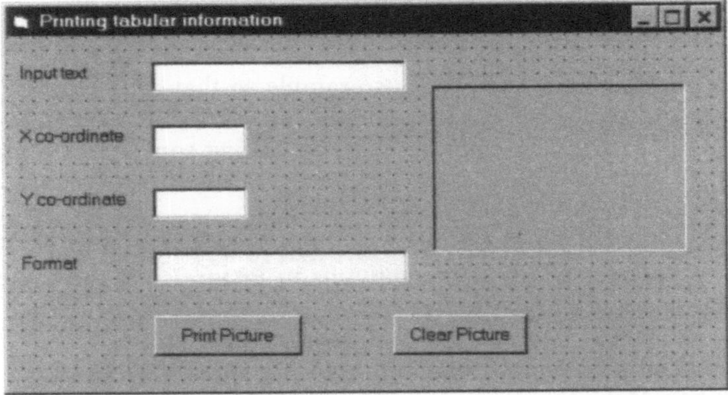

Fig. 21.20   *The design screen for printing tabular information.*

This form allows the user to enter some information, and choose the location at which it should be printed and the format it should be printed in.

When the form is loaded, set the text fields to valid values so that the print button can be used straight away. While the form is running:

- Ensure that the user information field is compatible with the format style before pressing the print button.
- As well as standard formats, e.g. long date or currency, try your own formats, e.g. £#,##0.000.
- Set the format field to a string of 'd's of varying lengths to see the effect that it has on the printed format.
- Set the format field to a string of 'm's of varying lengths to see the effect that it has on the printed format.
- Set the format field to a string of 'y's of varying lengths to see the effect that it has on the printed format.

The Scribble Program

This exercise supports Chapter 17.

The aim is to write a program that will allow you to scribble using the mouse (fig. 21.21).

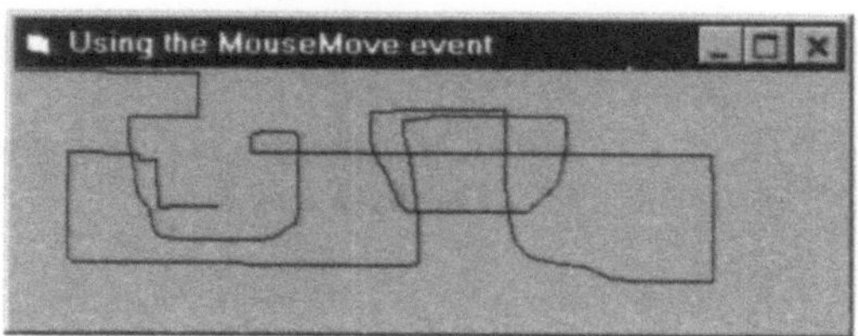

Fig. 21.21
Using the **MouseMove** event.

When the mouse moves, an event occurs; since only a limited number of events are generated by the operating system per second, not every pixel touched signals an event.

This program is only one line long!

Modify the program so that it does not always start drawing its lines from the top left corner of the form.

Using Navigation Keys

This program uses the **KeyDown** events to drive an icon around the form.

Create a picture box control and insert the picture BICYCLE.ICO into it.

The position of the picture on the form is determined by the control's properties of **Top, Bottom, Left** and **Right**.

The program should respond to the depression of the arrowed keys by moving the picture 100 twips in the specified direction. It will do this by changing the **Top** property if the up arrow is pressed, and so on.

Note: The **KeyPress** event cannot be used, since this can only be operated to test for input from keys that generate ASCII characters.

File Handling

This exercise supports Chapters 19 and 20.

This program uses three controls:

- **DriveListBox** control
- **DirListBox** control
- **FileListBox** control.

The aim is to use these three controls to find the file HELLO.TXT, to read it and to display the result in a message box. You will need to create this file using any text editor.

- Create a new project.
- Create a form using the **DriveListBox**, the **DirListBox** and the **FileListBox** controls (fig. 21.22).

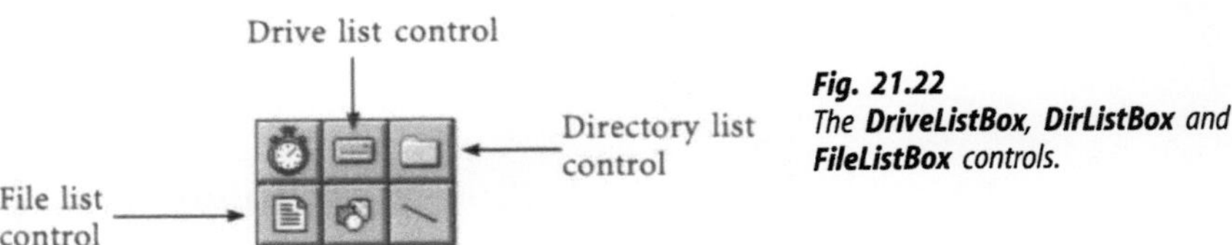

Fig. 21.22
The **DriveListBox**, **DirListBox** and **FileListBox** controls.

Your form should be similar to the one shown in fig. 21.23.

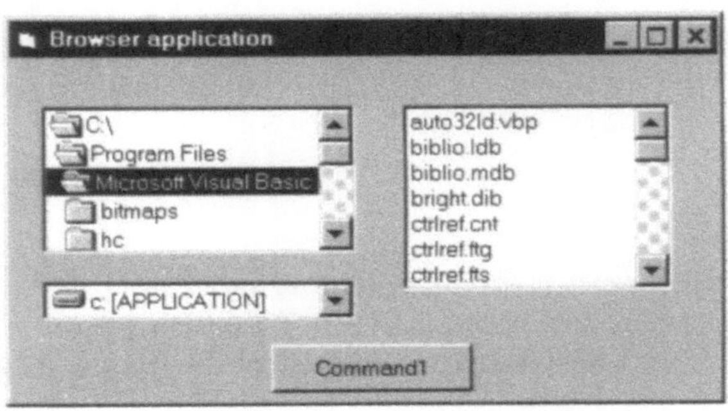

Fig. 21.23
The running browser application.

In order for the changes in the drive selected to be reflected in the directories displayed, you will need to use the **Path** property.

The **Path** property determines the current absolute path, including the drive name. The **Path** property is a string, for example, "D:/VISUALB/HELLO.TXT". **Path** can be used with the file and directory list boxes to change the directory and files displayed.

For a **DriveListBox** control, the name of the drive will be *drive1.Drive.* The current disk drive used by the **DirListBox** is *dir1.Path.* This can be changed to reflect the new disk drive by putting the statement

> *dir1.Path = drive1.Drive*

into the procedure that processes the drive-selected event (this is reached by double clicking on the **DriveListBox** control).

Similarly the current directory used by the file **FileListBox** control is given by File1.**Path**. This can be changed to reflect that selected by the **DirListBox** control box by the statement:

> *File1.Path = dir1.Path.*

- Locate the file "HELLO.TXT".
- Open it for reading and read the text.
- Display the text you have read in a dialog box when the button is pressed.

This application can also be done using the **CommonDialog** control – you need to write even less code if you use this control.

Christmas Present Database

The aim of this exercise is to write a program that will allow you to enter a list of names, the Christmas presents you are buying for each person and the cost.
The form you generate will resemble the one shown in fig. 21.24.

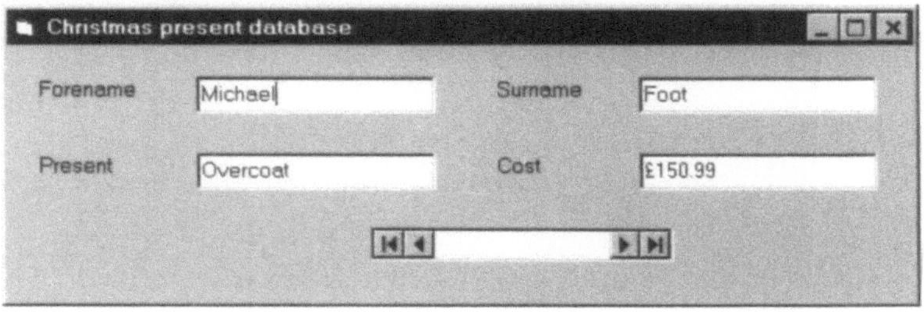

Fig. 21.24   *The Christmas present database.*

- Create a new project.
- Create a form similar to the one shown in fig. 21.24.
- Create an access database using the database manager which contains one table.

The table contains the following data items:

- *Forename*   20 characters
- *Surname*   20 characters
- *Present*   40 characters
- *Cost*   currency
- Enter (say) five people in the table.
- Connect the data control to the application.
- Bind the individual controls to the database.

When the program is run, you will be able to view the information entered by using the data control.

Index